BUYING FREEDOM

BUYING FREEDOM: THE ETHICS AND ECONOMICS OF SLAVE REDEMPTION

Edited by Kwame Anthony Appiah
and Martin Bunzl

With a foreword by Kevin Bales

PRINCETON UNIVERSITY PRESS   PRINCETON AND OXFORD

Contents

Foreword

KEVIN BALES

This multidimensional exploration of redemption is exciting, intriguing, and deeply hopeful. Slave redemption has been a controversial subject for centuries, and the controversies that have surrounded it in the past and surround it today are themselves multifaceted. Morality, economics, politics, and the proper strategies and tactics for eradicating slavery generally, all have a part in the comprehension of this issue. As often happens when lives are at stake, the discussion over redemption has, at times, become polarized, even vicious. Clarity of thought is not enhanced by passion, but when confronting monolithic systems of terror and exploitation, the passionate and single-minded adherence to one path of action may be seen as the only chance of success.

I have had the uncomfortable good fortune of experiencing this controversy in person. For some fifteen years I have been exploring firsthand the ideas of slave liberation and redemption, and at the same time living in the global laboratory where these ideas are being tested. Looking into the faces of slaves, it was sometimes difficult to know the correct path of action—what intervention would be most likely to lead to a successful liberation and rehabilitation? It was always clear that a broad and careful analysis of redemption was needed. That this need might be met is the basis of the hope I feel underpins this book. There are still some 27 million of slaves in the world today. Over the next decades, many thousands of these slaves and free people may find that their lives intersect as some benefit from and others support redemption. While this book does not provide an answer to the question of redemption in any individual's case, it extends and deepens our understanding of the subject, and makes it more likely that we can respond to the lived experience of slaves in ways that do the least harm, and perhaps opens the opportunity for liberation and true autonomy.

As an example of the guidance that is so very needed, let me point to the chapter by Kellow. Working with the original and oldest anti-slavery organization, Anti-Slavery International, and establishing its sister organization in the United States, Free the Slaves, in the late 1990s, I was directly confronted with the question of real slaves. There were significant and sometimes potentially damaging consequences for slaves, the organizations, and myself, consequences that were linked to the possible

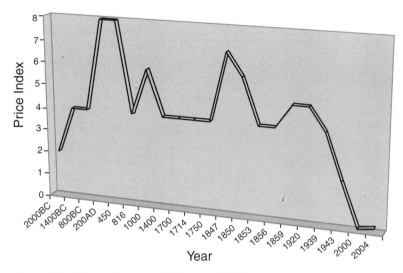

Figure F.1 Price of slaves 2000 BC to 2004 AD.

items, today their price has fallen to the same level as many goods seen to be "disposable." Figure F.1 shows this collapse in the price of slaves. The price index is not based on monetary costs of slaves, but on the relationship of the price of slaves to the prices of oxen, productive land, and free agricultural labor over time. For example, if the cost of a slave was approximately equal to that of five oxen or the cost of hiring a free agricultural worker for fifteen months in the United States in 1856 (represented by a score of 4 on the price index in fig. F.1), the price of a slave has fallen to one-sixth of an ox in modern India, or 4 percent of the annual wages of a free farm worker in the Ivory Coast today. I point to this fall in price because of the importance it could have for economic analyses of all forms of enslavement, including the analysis of redemption.

Because most slavery today is part of a hidden economy, and because in Sudan in particular buyers could be ignorant of price trends, models that assume a general level of shared knowledge need careful examination. This is especially the case for models comparing the relatively open economic system of the antebellum South with that of Sudan in the late twentieth century. Slave prices were general knowledge and public record in the United States in the 1850s. But what did redemptionists flying into southern Sudan in the 1990s know of the price of a slave in Khartoum? What did they know of historical pricing of slaves in money, goods, or livestock in the rounds of capture and redemption played out between the southern ethnic groups? Might there have been two parallel price systems in effect, one for "consumers" of slaves and one for "redeemers"? In the return of many of those abducted and enslaved, it becomes more possible to collect that information.

As those that were enslaved return from northern Sudan, related questions of rehabilitation and reintegration arise. Engerman, in his chapter, provides an important discussion of the experience of American slaves after emancipation. The process of enslavement and liberation should not be characterized as events, but processes, often lifelong. Our understanding of the needs of ex-slaves is as sketchy today as our understanding of redemption has previously been. In the work of my own organization, with our partners overseas, we are engaged in the liberation of slaves in many ways, sometimes through force, sometimes through aided escape, and sometimes through fostering the social, economic, and political changes that enable slave communities to liberate themselves. A constant concern is to support ex-slaves in attaining economic autonomy and the rights of citizenship. The lack of research on the processes of rehabilitation and reintegration means that we often feel we are flying blind, but we are motivated by the knowledge that the botched emancipation of 1865 and its tragic aftermath carried the crippling legacy of slavery into subsequent generations. This is an outcome we are determined never to replicate. In some areas, particularly northern India, we have developed systems that seem to be generally successful at both liberation and reintegration, but with the numbers of freed slaves increasing we look to others to carry out the research that will illuminate this process and help academics and practitioners comprehend its complexities.

Ongoing work against slavery around the world, including the tens of thousands of cases of enslavement in North America, means that the question of redemption is not one of simple historical or academic interest. While the scale of slave redemption in Sudan drew the attention of the public and academics alike, it was not an isolated instance. Today, in many countries and situations, the possibility exists to enter into an economic transaction that will lead to a radical transformation, for better or worse, of a person's status as a slave, bonded worker, or forced laborer. The World Bank has supported a number of projects using "conditional cash transfers" to remove children from the workforce, and it would be a small step to consider using the same approach with children (or adults) in slavery. This volume considers areas of the world in addition to Sudan, such as McDougall's work on French West Africa. We should build upon the work of this book to further expand our view of redemption to include its many possible forms and manifestations. Many of these forms will fit better to economic models in that they are not played out in a context of conflict.

Introduction

KWAME ANTHONY APPIAH AND MARTIN BUNZL

This volume has its origins in an unsolicited telemarketing call. One of us (MB) was asked for money to (purportedly) free a slave in Sudan and was intrigued enough to solicit views from a variety of human rights and international relief organizations. Struck by the near unanimous condemnation of the practice, the editors began an extended conversation with others about just what (if only under idealized circumstances) would make such a practice morally wrong. We began with a small meeting at the Center for Human Values at Princeton, where we brought together a multidisciplinary group of philosophers, anthropologists, and economists, to begin thinking about these questions. Since then we have carried our discussions further and enlarged our numbers, continuing to exchange and develop our ideas.

The results of the conversations prompted by the original practical question are represented in what follows. When we began this endeavor we thought of this as primarily a philosophical exercise. And indeed there are traditional arguments that can and have been marshaled against the practice of buying others even if it is to grant them their freedom. A UNICEF spokesperson captures the deontological cast of such arguments well in objecting that a buy-back program implicitly accepts that human beings may be bought and sold (Peter Crowley as reported by Lewis 1999). More broadly, it might be thought that, irrespective of the good consequences that might follow, buying human beings treats them as a commodity and therefore not as an end in themselves. Such arguments also figured large in some of the nineteenth-century debates (both in the African-American community and among Quakers) that Margaret Kellow takes up in chapter 9. Howard McGary assesses the philosophical merits of such arguments in chapter 11.

That said, the vast majority of objections to buy-back programs have a decidedly more consequentialist cast. And consequentialist arguments often stand or fall on the underlying facts that they ride on. In this case, what they ride on is a matter of economics. Most people have a strong intuition that to enter the market for slaves will raise demand, thereby pushing up prices, which will draw more people into the slave trade, resulting in more people being enslaved. That looks like a classic case of helping the one but hurting the many (more). And such an intuition underlies the objections of a number of organizations (including UNICEF and Human Rights Watch, as Kreuger and Karlan point out in chapter 1).

the significance of attempts to end slavery from the "outside" without understanding its local cultural history. In chapter 8, Lisa Cook examines whether or not there are lessons to be learned from the emancipation of serfs in Russia that might be applied to modern cases of slavery.

Notwithstanding these complexities, historically, opposition to slave redemption, even when held as a matter of principle, runs up against the contingencies of practice. This tension is discussed in chapter 9 by Margaret Kellow in her account of debates about redemption in both the nineteenth-century African-American and Quaker communities. Even where redemption was practiced, just under what description it was to be understood turned out to be crucial, as John Stauffer points out (in chapter 10) in his treatment of Frederick Douglass's view of the purchase of his freedom by British Quakers.

Suppose redeeming a slave helps the one and does not hurt the many. And suppose we answer objections to the implicit commodification of human life involved in such transactions. Still, ought we not to consider if we could do greater good by helping others instead—say the starving? But as Martin Bunzl argues (in chapter 12), such interests ought to be tempered by attention to just how likely it is that such prescriptive advice will actually be followed, even if doing so would produce a greater good than freeing a slave.

The last chapter contains reflections by Anthony Appiah on the moral significance of slavery. He argues that once we understand what is wrong with slavery we will see that legal emancipation is only the beginning of a process of freeing the enslaved from the consequences of the combination of low status and minimal autonomy that are at the heart of the evil of enslavement.

Despite its breadth of scope, this volume was conceived during and prompted by consideration of the conflict in southern Sudan. Whether the recent end of this conflict represents a permanent cessation of hostilities remains to be seen. But as Jok Madut Jok points out in his poignant summaries of his interviews with Sudanese abductees in the appendix, even if the conflict is over (although perhaps just relocated to the Darfur region), the formerly enslaved will continue to pay the cost of slavery for the remainder of their lives.

In this volume, we take ourselves to be addressing the question of the ethics of buying the freedom of an enslaved person. Just how many slaves there are in the world today is a function of how narrowly or broadly one construes the term. We tend to think of slavery as a relationship in which ownership is involved because of the centrality of ownership to the history of slavery in the United States. But as Kevin Bales points out, historically, many forms of slavery lacked such a component. Bales

decision, once we have the advice in hand, involves balancing a wide variety of considerations. And in the real world that balancing can be very difficult.

Bibliography

Anti-Slavery Society (no date), http://www.anti-slaverysociety.addr.com/slavery3 .htm.

Bales, Kevin (1999), *Disposable People*. Berkeley: University of California Press.

Bales, Kevin (2000), *The New Slavery*. Santa Barbara: ABC-CLIO.

Lewis, Paul (1999), "U.N. Criticism Angers Charities Buying Sudan Slaves' Release," *New York Times*, March 12.

Part I

THE ECONOMICS OF REDEMPTION

Chapter One

Some Simple Analytics of Slave Redemption

DEAN S. KARLAN AND ALAN B. KRUEGER

THE IDEA OF purchasing the freedom of slaves is not new. Alexander Hamilton, for example, helped found the Society for Promoting the Manumission of Slaves in New York in 1785, and raised money to buy and free slaves (see Randall 2003). The Pennsylvania Abolition Society and Quaker groups likewise purchased the freedom of a significant number of slaves. Even earlier, in the sixteenth century, the church issued orders to raise a considerable sum of money to redeem the freedom of Spanish and Portuguese captives held as slaves in North Africa (Eltis 1993).

Despite the long historical precedent, slave redemption remains a controversial response to the horrible practice of slavery. Two types of slave redemption programs exist, ones that merely attempt to free a certain number of slaves, and ones that are part of a concerted effort to free all slaves and forever stop future slavery in the area. In this chapter, we primarily discuss the former. The United Nations Children's Fund (UNICEF) considers slave redemption efforts "absolutely intolerable" and has condemned the practice in the Sudan (Lewis 1999). UNICEF makes two claims, that purchasing slaves' freedom for money (1) exacerbates the slave trade, and (2) does not address the root of the problem. Human Rights Watch (2002) also has denounced slave redemptions in the Sudan, citing concerns that monetary incentives could lead to more raiding of free Dinkas, although the organization acknowledges, "It has not been possible to date to ascertain whether the monetary incentive produced more raiding in practice." The group also raises the valid concern that some of those who have been redeemed were not actually slaves.

There seems to us little doubt that redemption efforts do not address the root of the problem unless accompanied by more systematic emancipation and enforcement policies. This acknowledgment is not necessarily dispositive vis-à-vis slave redemption programs, however. From a practical standpoint one could still be interested in whether a redemption program reduces the number of slaves in captivity. This is the primary question analyzed here.

Here we apply conventional economic tools to analyze the likely effects of a slave redemption program on the quantity of slaves in captivity.

demand for slave services. The supply of slaves in a specified period of time will depend on the cost of capturing slaves and delivering them to market, which would include any social stigma associated with being a slave supplier. The demand for slaves by potential slaveowners will depend on the value of the output that slaves produce net of monitoring and enforcement costs, boarding costs, and any stigma associated with owning slaves. The interaction of the supply and demand determines the price at which slaves are traded and the number of slaves that are bought and sold.

In a competitive market, the supply curve is determined by the marginal cost of supplying a good to the market. The supply curve for slaves likely slopes upward, as it is likely to be more costly to provide another slave to the market than it was to capture and deliver the previous slave to the market. That is, the easiest to capture, most productive slaves are captured first. On the margin, the next 100 slaves supplied to the market are likely to be more costly to provide than the previous 100. If it were costless to capture slaves—and there were enough slave providers to generate competition—the price of a slave in equilibrium would be zero because the market would be flooded with slaves.

Figure 1.1 illustrates the equilibrium in the slave market. The supply curve is upward sloping because, as just discussed, the marginal cost of capturing and delivering slaves is likely to be rising with the number of slaves in captivity. We will return to the polar case of an infinitely elastic (or horizontal) supply curve for slaves shortly. The demand curve is downward sloping because the demand for slaves is a derived demand, dependent on the amount of output produced by slaves. As is standard in economics—and particularly likely to hold in the agricultural markets where slaves are often forced to work—we assume that there is declining marginal productivity of labor, which necessitates that the demand curve is downward sloping.

The equilibrium (meaning the price and quantity of slaves traded that the market tends toward) is determined by the intersection of the supply and demand curves. The equilibrium price is P* and the equilibrium quantity is Q* slaves in captivity. This figure assumes an implicit set of institutions similar to those that were in place in the United States in the antebellum period—there was an active slave market in which slaves were brought to market, and slaves were exchanged at a market-determined price. To focus on a redemption program, the figure abstracts from differences in prices for slaves with different attributes, and treats slaves as homogeneous as far as slaveowners are concerned.

Next we introduce a redemption program. We interpret a redemption program as follows: An outside organization steps in and purchases the freedom of X slaves, regardless of their price. After they are freed, the

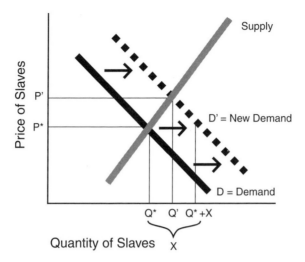

Figure 1.2 Demand and supply for slaves with a slave redemption program.

in price. A flat supply curve corresponds to an infinite elasticity of supply. So a key concept is the supply elasticity. A redemption program will be more successful in situations where the supply curve is less elastic. It will be completely ineffective if the elasticity of supply is infinite. In the section "Cost Function" we will discuss how to think about determining whether the elasticity of supply is infinite.[1]

Notice another implication of the model: the price of slaves traded will rise with a redemption program if the supply elasticity is finite. This can be monitored. Thus, a more successful program will raise the price of slaves. This should be viewed as a positive result, as a higher price will discourage current slaveowners from owning slaves; they would rather sell them to the redeemers. Ironically, the consequence of "raising the price of slaves" is often cited as a reason to *oppose* slave redemption, yet a higher price is exactly the sign one would expect if the intervention has reduced the number of slaves held in captivity; indeed, it is the mechanism by which slave ownership is reduced.

The slope of the demand curve is also relevant. The slope of the demand curve reflects the responsiveness of slaveowners to a change in the cost of acquiring slaves. If the demand curve of slaveowners were a vertical line,

---

[1] If the demand curve were vertical, or perfectly inelastic, then the redemption program would not affect the number of slaves in captivity either. The reason for this is that demand is not sensitive to price. We suspect an inelastic demand curve is unlikely, however, in the sectors where slaves are commonly forced to work.

long after they are liberated. For example, Nicholas Kristof (2005) provides a wrenching report on two forced child prostitutes whose freedom he purchased, one of whom was unable to readjust to life in her original village and voluntarily returned to prostitution. Bales (2004) provides much anecdotal evidence suggesting that many ex-slaves lead shattered lives, and often return to bondage. The fraction of freed slaves who are unable to adjust to their freedom, or whose lives are reduced to a shadow of what they otherwise would have been had they not been forced into slavery, is unknown but probably substantial.

The well-being of freed slaves is relevant because an unambiguous result of the theoretical model outlined in the previous section is that the number of people rotating through the state of slavery will increase under a slave redemption program. Thus, the number of people who were *ever* forced into slavery would be increased in a slave redemption program. If being forced to work as a slave, even briefly, leaves a permanent scar on individuals, then the purchase of slaves' freedom can lower welfare.

Cost Function: The Origin of the Supply Curve

The prior analysis suggests that an estimate of the elasticity of supply is essential for estimating the likely impact of a slave redemption program on the number of slaves held in captivity. The supply elasticity depends critically on the institutional setting and the particulars of slavery in a given society. In a competitive market, the supply curve is simply the marginal cost of capturing and delivering slaves to the market. The cost structure of supplying adult slaves in the Sudan for agricultural or household labor clearly is different than that of supplying child prostitute slaves in Southeast Asia, and different than that of supplying indentured servitudes "voluntarily." We attempt here to provide some examples and structure to organize how one might think about estimating the relevant cost curve.

We will discuss costs for two types of suppliers, households (e.g., indentured servitude, where a household sells a family member in order to satisfy a debt) and slave entrepreneurs (e.g., a slave trader who captures individuals by force and sells them to others for farm, domestic, factory, or prostitution labor). We start with the case of the household. The cost of supplying an additional household member to the slave market is the sum of the lost stream of revenue (through either household production, wages, or self-employment income) from that individual, plus the emotional cost of selling that individual and losing his or her company. The moral, emotional, and/or social stigma costs clearly are harder if not impossible to quantify, and for the sake of analysis we assume this to be

setting a portion of them free, a slave redemption program will drive up the price of slaves supplied to the market and discourage some slave-owners from holding slaves as long as the elasticity of supply is finite.

To assess the merits of these arguments, one would need two types of data: the price at which slaves are exchanged (ideally before and after redemption programs) and the number of slaves in captivity (again, ideally before and after a redemption program). Additionally, data allowing estimation of the shape of the cost function for supplying slaves to the market would provide useful information for determining whether a slave redemption program is likely to be efficacious by enabling an estimate of the elasticity of supply.

Monitoring prices of slaves before and after a slave redemption program is implemented provides an indirect indication of the effectiveness of the program. If the price is unchanged, then either the program was too small to have any detectable effect or the supply curve was very elastic. Unless the slave market is organized and open, as it was in antebellum America, for instance, monitoring prices may be very difficult.

Still, even if data on prices are unavailable, it may be possible to collect data on costs of capturing and delivering slaves to slaveholders. As discussed above, the relevant costs depend entirely on the institutional setting of the slave market in the country of interest. For those settings in which households decide, due to abject poverty or other reasons, to sell their kin into slavery, detailed data on household production might provide some insight into the shape of the supply curve, and the likely effectiveness of a redemption program.

Of course, slave redemption could be considered morally repugnant because it requires the purchase of slaves, which could be viewed as condoning the slave trade, and it transfers resources to those who capture and sell slaves. But, just as paying cash for high-emission cars does not indicate approval of air pollution, we think a case could be made that purchasing the freedom of slaves is a noble act. However, one would want to be sure that the net effects of the program are positive, and that the limited resources that are available for slave purchases are used in the situations where they have the greatest positive impact for welfare. The simple model we provided gives a framework for considering the effects and effectiveness of slave redemption initiatives.

Another consideration is whether slave redemption diverts attention, energy, and resources of the international community from alternative means of reducing or abolishing forced labor. Slave redemption is clearly a short-term solution, where the ultimate goal is the complete abolition of slavery. Slave redemption programs can help to make slavery uneconomical for slaveowners by driving up the cost of slaveownership, however, and therefore help to hasten its end.

Kristof, Nicholas (2005), "Back to the Brothel," *New York Times*, 22 January 2005, A15.

Lewis, Paul (1999), "U.N. Criticism Angers Charities Buying Sudan Slaves' Release," *New York Times*, 12 March 1999, A7.

Madison, James (1819), "Letter to Robert J. Evans, author of the pieces published under the name of Benjamin Rush," 15 June 1819.

Randall, Williard Sterne (2003), *Alexander Hamilton: A Life*, New York: HarperCollins.

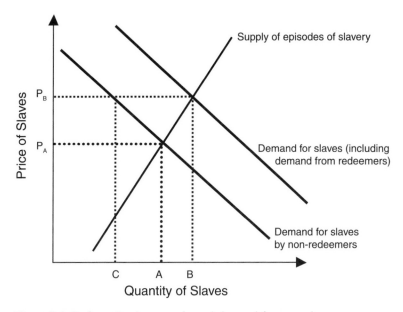

Figure 2.1 Redemption in a supply-and-demand framework.

of slavery that occur depends on the market price of slaves. The inner-most downward-sloping curve is the demand curve from nonredeemers. This curve shows how the number of slaves held by those who demand slaves for use as slave labor depends on the market price of slaves. Before the institution of a slave redemption program, the equilibrium price of slaves is P_A, and the number of episodes of slavery is the same as the number of people demanded and enslaved, i.e., the quantity at point A. The redemption program demands BC slaves, so that the total demand for slaves becomes the demand generated by those who buy slaves with the intention of using them as such, *plus* the demand of the redeemers who intend to free the slaves they buy. The market demand curve becomes the outermost downward-sloping curve. The supply of slaves must be at least equal to the number of slaves actually bought, and so even though the redemption program leads to a decline in the number of people held in slavery to point C, it also must lead to an increase in the number, to point B, of people who suffer an episode of slavery. In this framework, it must also lead to an increase in the price at which slaves are exchanged, i.e., from P_A to P_B.

A Matching Model of Slave Redemption

The supply-and-demand model does not explicitly discuss the factors that affect the time it will take to achieve the predicted reduction in the

each buyer and redeemer seeks to buy just one slave. These assumptions simplify the exposition of the matching model, but are not essential to our conclusions, which remain valid if more than one slave can be exchanged at a time.

The first thing a slave raider needs to do is to capture a slave to sell. Adopting the assumption that generated the upward-sloping supply curve in the supply-and-demand model, we assume that the cost of capturing a slave is a function of the aggregate number of slaves offered by slave raiders, and that this cost increases with the number offered. Call this function $C(S)$. Note that this cost is "sunk" at the time of capture.

After securing a slave to offer, a slave raider must find someone to buy the slave. For the moment, we assume that there are no redeemers and just concentrate on how a slave raider achieves an exchange with a buyer. We avoid a discussion of the many ways that a slave raider may search for a buyer and instead follow the convention in matching models of positing that in any given period of time, a slave raider has some probability of success, q, of finding a buyer. This probability is related to the level of aggregate activity in the market for slaves. To capture this, we posit the existence of a function, $q\left(\dfrac{B}{S}\right)$ where B stands for the total number of buyers searching for one slave each and S for the number of slave raiders looking for buyers. The probability that an individual slave raider is matched with a buyer is thus a function of the ratio of the aggregate number of buyers to slave raiders in the market. It is natural to assume that as there are more buyers per slave raider, the probability that a slave raider will find a buyer goes up, so that q increases as $\dfrac{B}{S}$ increases. Nevertheless, a slave raider is never absolutely certain to find a buyer in a given period of time, so q is always strictly less than one.

The average time it takes a slave raider to sell a slave is related to the probability, q, that a slave raider finds a buyer in a given period of time. To see how, suppose that q is the probability of finding a buyer in one month, and that this probability is one in 12. With the monthly probability of meeting a buyer at $\dfrac{1}{12}$, the seller expects to wait 12 months to find a buyer. As this example implies, generally, the expected time to sale of a slave is the inverse of the probability of sale; therefore, from the time that a slave raider secures a slave to sell, he expects it to take $\dfrac{1}{q}$ periods to find a buyer for that slave.

When the raider and buyer meet, they must negotiate a price at which the slave will be exchanged. Assuming the slave raider incurs no per-period costs to support a slave, so that there are no costs to be saved by unloading the slave, the payoff to the slave raider from selling a slave is

pay off is preferred to a later one: payoffs received in the future are discounted at rate i. This means that a payoff of p received one period in the future would have a present value of $p\left(\dfrac{1}{1+i}\right)$, a payoff of p received two periods in the future would have a present value of $p\left(\dfrac{1}{1+i}\right)^{2}$, and so forth. Since the expected amount of time until a slave raider is matched with a buyer and receives payoff p^{*} is equal to $\dfrac{1}{q\left(\dfrac{B}{S}\right)}$, the expected value of this payoff at the time the raider captures the slave is:

$$\textit{Expected present value of selling the slave} = p^{*}\left(\frac{1}{1+i}\right)^{\frac{1}{q\left(\frac{B}{S}\right)}}.$$

Let us simplify this expression by using the notation $F(B/S)$ to stand for the *discount factor* $\left(\dfrac{1}{1+i}\right)^{\frac{1}{q\left(\frac{B}{S}\right)}}$, so that the expected present value of selling the slave can be written as $p^{*}F(B/S)$. We note that this present value increases when the ratio of buyers to sellers increases. That is because the larger is this ratio, the higher is the probability that a seller finds a buyer in a given period of time, and the shorter is the length of time to a sale.

The expected present value is the same as the expected benefit, as of the time of capture, from capturing the slave. So long as this expected benefit exceeds the cost of capture, $C(S)$, raiding is expected to be a profitable endeavor, and more slave raiders will want to undertake the activity. In fact, absent binding restrictions on raiding activities, additional raiding will occur until the expected benefit of selling a slave is equal to the cost of capture—that is, until

$$p^{*}F\left(\frac{B}{S}\right) = C(S). \qquad \textit{(Equilibrium condition, no redeemers)}$$

Now let us assume that R redeemers enter this market. For the moment, let us also assume that they bargain in precisely the same way as other buyers, so that there is no change in the bargained price, i.e., it

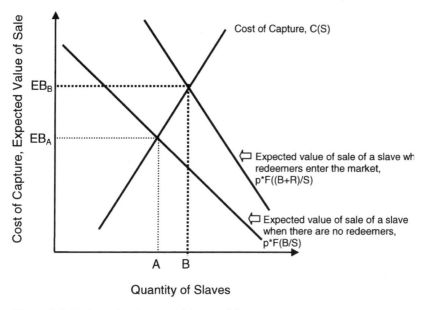

Figure 2.2 Redemption in a matching model.

number of people who suffer slavery, similar to the effect seen in figure 2.1. The move from *A* to *B* represents the increased capture of slaves due to redemption, and it represents an increase in the total number of slaves available for sale. We can also see from figure 2.2 that redemption programs cause the expected value from the sale of a slave to increase from EB_A to EB_B. Because we have assumed the price of slaves to be fixed in all instances at p^*, this is of a similar spirit to, but not the same as, the price effect shown in figure 2.1. In this example, the expected value goes up because redemption programs make the sale of slaves happen more quickly, *not because of changes in the price of a slave.*

In addition to the obvious contrast with the prediction about price from figure 2.1, this point may be of some practical relevance because one way in which redemption programs have been defended against concerns that they are having some negative impact is to point out that their activities have had no upward effect on the price of slaves exchanged. Jok Madut Jok (2001, 175) notes from his experience observing slavery in Sudan that the price at which slaves are exchanged remained at around $50 after the entry of international redeemers into the market. He also (176) cites one redeemer working in Sudan on behalf of Christian Solidarity International (CSI) who says he will not pay more than $50 for a slave, and will stop redeeming if the practice evolves into a "free market." Finally, Jok reviews arguments that suggest that local redeemers

and how many are redeemed. While figure 2.2 does not aid in making this determination, it is possible to use the equilibrium equation on which this figure is based to determine the *elasticity* of sales by slave raiders with respect to the number of redemptions. An elasticity is the percentage change in one variable (sales by slave raiders) with respect to a change of one percent in another (number of redemptions). If the elasticity of sales by slave raiders with respect to redemptions is greater than one, then more slaves are sold than are redeemed, implying that some of the slaves who are captured because of the redemption program must remain in slavery. If the elasticity is less than one, then more slaves are redeemed than were captured, implying that redemption ends more episodes of slavery than it creates, and the number of people left to flow into slavery falls.

The equilibrium equation (with redeemers) can be shown to imply that the elasticity of slave raiding with respect to redemptions is less than one. In terms of figure 2.2, this means that while redemption programs induce *AB* more episodes of slavery, they redeem more than *AB* slaves. Intuitively, this is for two reasons. The first is that since capturing an additional slave raises the cost of capturing still more, there is a natural brake on the number of new episodes of slavery. The second reason is that the redemption programs raise the opportunity cost of holding onto a slave to look for a buyer because the expected value of selling a slave decreases as the date to sale is put off. Because rising costs of capture tend to discourage more capture, and because rising opportunity costs tend to discourage waiting for buyers, the net effect of slave redemption programs is to cause the number of people sold to buyers to fall, even though the programs cause more people to be captured by slave raiders.

From the perspective of the people who suffer through slavery, the important social welfare trade-off to evaluate is whether reducing the number of people who enter into longer-term slavery is worth exposing more people to the capture that creates the supply of potential slaves. Two questions seem relevant to the evaluation of this trade-off. The first is, how long are the redemption-induced captives held by slave raiders? The answer to this is that the time to redemption for any slave redeemed should be, on average, $\frac{1}{q}$ periods. The second is, what is the nature of the experience of an eventually redeemed captive while waiting to be redeemed? We discuss this question in the next section.

Costs Associated with Redemption-Induced Episodes of Slavery

Unless the price at which slaves are exchanged rises so high that all slaveholders would rather sell their slaves than hold on to them, both the supply-and-demand and the matching models unambiguously predict

slaves by claiming it to be an act of mercy. . . . The slavers are often convinced that they are doing a favor for the captives; they regard the Dinka culture as inferior and believe that these Southerners are fortunate to have been incorporated into a superior culture. This is the kind of explanation that has caused some historians to describe early slavery in the Muslim world as benign. Some writers are doing the same regarding present-day slavery in Sudan.

A courteous treatment of slaves, undoubtedly, makes slavery more acceptable to the northern society and sometimes to the slaves who were caught at a very young age and incorporated into northern culture and religion. But this does not make it less than slavery. A slave is a slave. Moreover, the current Sudanese slavery is less an economic practice than a cultural project, because there are many poor Baggara who hold slaves that often live no worse than their master.

Inasmuch as this quotation suggests that the daily life of being a slave once one has been a slave for awhile may be less harsh than what one suffers early in one's tenure of being a slave, it suggests a reason to be more worried about the costs that may be inflicted on redemption-induced slaves, than the benefits produced by securing the saving of other slaves.

Slave redemption did occur during this time in Sudan, and it spurred great controversy. Some of the controversy was specifically about whether or not redemption programs encouraged more raiding for slaves (see, e.g., Miniter 1999, and Human Rights Watch 2002). In response to concerns that they did or could, one group of redeemers, Christian Solidarity International (2002) issued a statement that said, in part:

> The fact is that since 1998, while CSI has redeemed increasing numbers of slaves, the number of slave raids and the number of women and children taken into bondage have diminished. This trend has been confirmed by the independent UN Special Rapporteur for Sudan, Gerhart Baum[,] in his most recent report to the UN Commission for Human Rights.

What the CSI statement does not acknowledge, but what is clear from reading many of the other already cited sources, including those from the United Nations, is that there were a variety of other initiatives taking place in the Sudan at the time aimed at reducing raiding, and it is not at all clear that CSI is justified in the causal implication this passage suggest. Returning to the view from the model of the previous section, the fact that redeemers apparently did not cause an increase in the price of slaves suggests another reason to be skeptical that redemption led to a decrease in raiding activities. We tend to share the view of Jok (2001, 175) that there is no empirical evidence to evaluate the true impact of slave redemption is essentially the same as for the trafficking example discussed earlier. Our concern now is with the case when entry and exit are purely voluntary.[1]

Again we turn to our model to provide some insights on the risk of redemption programs in these situations. This time, there are no slave raiders, but for theoretical purposes, we can treat a voluntary slave as a self raider. When the perceived benefit they expect to enjoy from entering prostitution exceeds the perceived cost of doing so, they enter. Note that the upward-sloping $C(S)$ curve in figure 2.2 suggests that as more and more victims make themselves available, the cost of purchasing them rises. This is because the latest victims to enter will likely require a higher payoff to do so than the earlier ones. A redemption program increases the number of victims who make themselves available for, but decreases the number who actually enter, prostitution. In this instance, a redemption program provides the victims who participate with a better option than prostitution. Since the offering of this option causes more people to choose to leave than choose to enter, and since "victims" in all instances make choices, we may be least concerned about "up-front" costs associated with redemption programs in these instances.

Concluding Remarks

In this chapter we analyzed slave redemption programs in a simple matching model. Unlike in a simple supply-and-demand framework, where sufficiently large and effective redemption programs must lead to an increase in the price at which slaves are exchanged, we find that such programs have no necessary impact on price. We also demonstrate that a slave redemption program can slow the flow of people into the actual state of slavery, but at the same time can increase the number of people captured to be slaves. We discussed redemption programs in the context of three contemporary examples of slavery. This discussion suggests that the risk of harming someone in the name of helping someone else appears

---

[1] We take a moment to emphasize our intended meaning of the word "voluntary" in this context, and the implication of our definition. By voluntary, we mean that no one has kidnapped or imprisoned the child who becomes or remains a prostitute, and that the child could leave at any time. Some may object to this definition by arguing that the child is "forced" by circumstance: she may have no other choice but to become a prostitute, *if* she wishes to survive. But then the tragedy is not so much that she has chosen prostitution, as it is that the only choice available to her is between prostitution and death. Whereas legal prohibitions all by themselves can improve the lot of children who are stolen into and imprisoned in prostitution, they will harm the child who is prostituted because she has no better choice, *unless* better choices are also provided to her. Eliminating voluntary prostitution therefore *requires* that attention be paid not only to the fact that the child is a prostitute, but also to making sure that she has better choices available.

feasible policy options. In some full social welfare accounting, informed not only by economics but also by ethics, the benefits of slave redemption may outweigh the costs. But it certainly is also wise to consider, and more extensively than we have the opportunity to do here, the possibility that some other program might generate equal benefit at lower cost.[2]

Bibliography

Azaola, Elena (2000), *Stolen Childhood: Girl and Boy Victims of Sexual Exploitation in Mexico*. Mexico City: DIF/UNICEF/CIESAS.

Bales, Kevin (1999), *Disposable People*. Berkeley: University of California Press.

Christian Solidarity International (2002), "Christian Solidarity International Statement on Slave Redemption Work in Sudan," http://iabolish.com/redemption/CSI-60.htm.

Human Rights Watch (2002), "Slavery and Slave Redemption in the Sudan, Human Rights Watch Backgrounder," http://www.hrw.org/backgrounder/africa/sudanupdate.htm.

International Labor Organization (1999), *Convention Concerning the Prohibition and Immediate Action for the Elimination of the Worst Forms of Child Labor (No. 182), 1999,* adopted by the International Labor Conference at its 87th session, 17 June 1999, Geneva.

Jok, Madut Jok (2001), *War and Slavery in Sudan*, Philadelphia: University of Pennsylvania Press.

Miniter, Richard (1999), "The False Promise of Slave Redemption," *Atlantic Monthly*, 284(1), July, pp. 63–70.

Pissarides, Christopher A. (1990), *Equilibrium Unemployment Theory*, Oxford: Basil Blackwell Ltd.

Report of the International Eminent Persons Group (2002), "Slavery, Abduction and Forced Servitude in Sudan," http://www.state.gov/p/af/rls/rpt/10445.htm.

Rogers, Carol Ann, and Kenneth A. Swinnerton (2004), "A Theory of Exploitative Child Labor," forthcoming in *Oxford Economic Papers*.

United Nations Commission on Human Rights (1994), *Situation of Human Rights in the Sudan: Report of the Special Rapporteur, Mr. Gáspár Bíró, submitted in Accordance with Commission on Human Rights Resolution 1993/60*, Geneva.

United Nations Commission on Human Rights (2004), *Report of the United Nations High Commissioner for Human Rights and Follow-Up to the World Conference on Human Rights: Situation of Human Rights in the Darfur Region of the Sudan*, Geneva.

United Nations General Assembly (1995), *Interim Report on the Situation of Human Rights in the Sudan prepared by Mr. Gáspár Bíró, Special Rapporteur*

[2] We thank Martin Bunzl for providing very helpful comments. The views presented in this paper are the personal views of the authors, and do not represent the official views of the U.S. Department of Labor.

Chapter Three

An Exploration of the Worst Forms of Child Labor: Is Redemption a Viable Option?

ARNAB K. BASU AND NANCY H. CHAU

Introduction

According to recent International Labor Organization (ILO) estimates, 211 million children between the ages of 5 and 14 are economically active, and of those, 186.3 million are child laborers.[1] In addition, 5.7 million children are in forced or bonded labor, 1.8 million in prostitution and 0.3 million in armed conflict. Table 3.1 provides a summary of the regional distribution of child labor and underscores the magnitude of the problem.

The extent of child labor varies regionally. Africa and the Middle East host approximately 30 percent of all economically active children worldwide. Meanwhile, the figure stands at around 60 percent in Asia (excluding Japan) and 8 percent in Latin America (including the Caribbean). Thus, in absolute terms, the incidence of child labor is highest in Asia (excluding Japan), as the most densely populated region of the world, with 127 million economically active children, compared to about 61 million in Africa and the Middle East and 17 million in Latin America (including the Caribbean). In addition, child labor can also be found in southern Europe and, increasingly, in the transitional economies of central and eastern Europe (ILO-IPEC 1997). However, in relative terms, sub-Saharan Africa ranks first when child labor prevalence is measured in terms of participation rates. In particular, approximately one out of every three children (or 29 percent) between 5 and 14 years of age are engaged in economic activities. In Asia about one in five children or 19 percent are part of the workforce, while in Latin America, one in six (or 16 percent).

---

[1] According to ILO terminology, a child who worked for one hour or more the previous week is economically active. A child laborer is defined as a child between the ages of 5 and 11 who is economically active, or one aged 12–14 who does 14 or more hours of nonhazardous work per week or 1 hour of hazardous work per week.

Child labor is not a new phenomenon. As Humphries (2003) points out, child labor was more prevalent in the nineteenth century in the newly industrializing countries of Britain, France, Belgium, western parts of Prussia, and the United States than in today's developing economies. Whereas Robert Peel's Factories Act of 1802 in Great Britain was widely recognized as the start of the decline in child labor, similar efforts by developing countries in the twenty-first century seemed to have had relatively little impact in eradicating the problem. These efforts include the ratification and adoption of a range of international legislation (such as the ILO Convention 138 concerning Minimum Age for Admission to Employment [1973], the UN Convention on the Rights of the Child [1989], and the ILO Convention 182 on the Elimination of the Worst Forms of Child Labour [1999]), in addition to domestic legislation by developing countries against child labor employment.

It has been frequently alleged that the lack of effectiveness of legislation to mitigate the child labor problem in developing countries has to do, at least in part, with lax enforcement of these laws, due either to a lack of resources or to corruption. But more importantly, it has also been argued that legislation *per se*, without an accompanying increase in the economic well-being of poor households (as was the case for much of newly industrialized western Europe and the United States), is unlikely to have any significant impact on the incidence of child labor. Indeed, the basic economic theory of child labor identifies poverty as the main reason altruistic households choose to send their children to work.

Basu and Van (1998) posit that if adult wages fall below a subsistence level, children will be sent to work to supplement household income in order to safeguard a minimum consumption level. Thus, it is possible for otherwise identical economies to exhibit drastically different child labor employment patterns, with high adult wages and no incidence of child labor in some countries, low adult wages and a high incidence of child labor in others.[2] In addition, the prevalence of low adult wages and high levels of child labor, if unchecked and allowed to impact the decision-making of individual households with regard to education, can also translate into low investment in human capital for current and future generations. A vicious cycle of poverty can thus ensue, with child labor serving as both the cause and the effect of the phenomenon. As the

---

[2] In recent years, economists have identified a host of market imperfections, for example lack of alternatives to child labor, i.e., education (Ranjan 2001; Grote, Basu, and Weinhold 1999), credit market failures that prevent poor households from borrowing to finance either education or consumption (Baland and Robinson 2000; Ranjan 1999; Basu and Chau 2003, 2004) and coordination failures on the part of households to bargain for higher wages (Basu and Chau 2003) as important factors in addition to poverty that lead to the emergence and persistence of child labor.

externalities, two specific types of the "worst forms of child labor," namely, child trafficking and child labor in debt bondage, have frequently been referred to as a form of forced labor or slavery, even though a child's ultimate involvement with these activities may have come from an *exante* "voluntary" agreement with a recruiter, employer, or landlord. We will now turn to a more in-depth look at these two forms of child labor. In consonance with the theme of this volume, our main focus will be on the efficacy of legislation that grants human rights (to those entrapped in these forms of slavery) on the incidence of the problem itself.

Worst Forms of Child Labor

As a matter of definition and identification, the ILO Convention on the Worst Forms of Child Labour (182) calls for the immediate suppression of all extreme forms of child labor including:

(a) all forms of slavery or practices similar to slavery, sale, trafficking of children, forced or compulsory labor including debt bondage and serfdom.
(b) the use, engagement, or offering of a child for the purposes of prostitution, production of pornography or pornographic performances, production of or trafficking in drugs or other illegal activities.
(c) the use or engagement of children in any type of work, which by its nature or the circumstances in which it is carried out, is likely to jeopardize their health, safety, or morals.[3]

Although the ILO's Convention on the Worst Forms of Child Labor has received the most international attention, there were two other earlier ILO conventions that specifically address the issue of slavery: 29, the Forced Labour Convention (1930), and 105, the Abolition of Forced Labour Convention (1957), which defines forced or compulsory labor as "all work or service which is extracted from any person under the menace of any penalty and for which the said person has not offered himself voluntarily." In addition to these ILO conventions, the United Nations specifically targets trafficking through its International Agreement for the Suppression of White Slave Traffic (1904),[4] while the United Nations Supplementary Convention on the Abolition of Slavery (1956) defines debt bondage as "the status or condition arising from a pledge by a debtor of his personal services or of those of a person under his control

---

[3] See Diller and Levy (1997) for an excellent survey of international conventions and laws governing child labor.
[4] See Dennis (2000) for a comprehensive treatment of UN and other international legislation regarding child labor.

types of child labor are distinct, they nevertheless share two common economic features that precipitate the problem—market imperfections and differential bargaining power amongst the concerned parties.

In the case of trafficking, market imperfection stems from incomplete information on the part of buyers of services from trafficked persons, who do not know how much to pay these workers. Meanwhile, potential sellers of services (the trafficked individuals) are likely imperfectly informed about the sort of work they will be engaged in and accordingly what sort of pay to expect. In the case of debt bondage, the market imperfection stems from the absence of a formal credit market that can insure poor households against income uncertainty.

In terms of bargaining power, the problem of trafficking is made worse as a larger number of uncoordinated and anonymous buyers and sellers are pitted against a small number of coordinated traffickers. Buyers lack bargaining power, since the consumption of services offered by trafficked individuals is illegal. The same lack of bargaining power also plagues potential sellers, who are unable to coordinate with each other due to their unmet income needs. Likewise for debt bondage, a large number of poor households who are unable to unionize and bargain for higher wages are typically faced with a small number of landlords-cum-moneylenders. In the case of trafficking, unequal bargaining power implies that traffickers reap most if not all of the rent generated from the *buyer-seller* match. For the case of debt bondage, unequal bargaining power implies that the structure of the debt service contract makes it particularly difficult for households to subsequently break free of bondage.

The economics of the worst forms of child labor, as seen through the lens of these two forms of market imperfections, underscores an additional issue that lies at the heart of the question of whether redemption can work: with multiple market imperfections, piecemeal policy reforms may well falter (Lipsey and Lancaster 1956). Redemption is of course an example of piecemeal reform, since it does not address the underlying sources of the child labor phenomenon. Thus, there is little guarantee that the granting of asylum to trafficked victims will not, for example, instigate a renewed surge in demand and supply of trafficked children. Likewise, simply paying off the debts of existing bonded child laborers does not release these children from the root cause of the phenomenon, ultimately having to do with the lack of access to credit and the lack of bargaining power in employment relations.

Put another way, the central question here is whether there are justifiable reasons to believe that the following two social objectives are competing rather than reinforcing: (i) freedom from slavery and serfdom as a human right for those who have been enslaved, and (ii) a sustainable decrease in the observed incidence of these two forms of

educational opportunities. In addition, armed conflict in some African countries such as Sierra Leone and Sudan gives rise to social fragmentation that makes it easier for children to be forcibly removed and trafficked by various factions. On the demand side, the largest demand for child trafficking and prostitution can be linked to the growth in income in both developed and developing countries. For developed countries, two factors are frequently alleged to be in play: (i) the rise of tourism from developed to developing countries and the subsequent rise in the demand for "sex tourism" as developed countries increasingly strengthen laws to protect minors and increase enforcement related to prostitution, and (ii) economic growth in developed countries, low fertility, and the subsequent increase in demand for cheap migrant labor. The latter effect is also evident in some developing countries that have witnessed relative prosperity over the last decade, and where the native population has gradually moved away from low-skilled, low-wage employment sectors. Consequently, migrants, legal and illegal, are now filling employment in these low-wage sectors. As an example, an increased number of children have migrated and/or have been trafficked into Thailand from Myanmar, Laos, and Cambodia to work in exploitative jobs previously done by Thai children (International Labour Organization 2002).

The pattern of trafficking and the types of work that trafficked individuals are engaged in vary across countries and continents. For instance, in Africa the most common source countries of trafficking are Sierra Leone, Malawi, Mozambique, Nigeria, and Somalia, from where children and women are trafficked to South Africa, Gabon, Gambia, and Western European countries primarily to work in the sex industry. There is also a steady supply of trafficked children from Mali to Côte d'Ivoire who end up working in cocoa plantations (UNICEF 2003). In Asia, the most common source countries of trafficking seem to be Bangladesh, Nepal, Vietnam, Bhutan, Laos, and Cambodia, while the host countries are India, Thailand, Sri Lanka, Saudi Arabia, United Arab Emirates (UAE), and Australia. Trafficked children and women are engaged in a variety of work. The primary activity remains prostitution, but an increasing number also work as domestic helpers in host countries, while young boys are smuggled from Bangladesh and India to work as camel jockeys in Saudi Arabia and the UAE (International Labour Organization 2002). In Central and South America, the source countries of trafficking are Bolivia, Colombia, Ecuador, and Honduras, and the host countries are Argentina, Belize, Mexico, El Salvador, and, in some cases, Guatemala, where trafficked women and children are usually coerced into prostitution. Similarly, trafficked women and children from the former republics of the Soviet Union (Estonia, Georgia, Ukraine, Uzbekistan, Kazakhstan and Kyrgyzstan) are usually forced

TABLE 3.3
List of Countries and Status of Trafficking

None	Host	Hub	Source
Andorra	Antigua	Afghanistan	Algeria
Bahamas	Australia	Albania	Angola
Barbados	Austria	Argentina	Armenia
Burundi	Belgium	Bahrain	Azerbaijan
Comoros	Belize	Bangladesh	Belarus
Croatia	Bosnia and Herzegovina	Benin	Bhutan
Djibouti	Botswana	Brazil	Bolivia
Egypt	Canada	Brunei	Cape Verde
Eritrea	Central African Republic	Bulgaria	Colombia
Fiji	Chile	Burkina Faso	Cuba
Iceland	Côte d'Ivoire	Cambodia	Ecuador
Jamaica	Denmark	Cameroon	Estonia
Lesotho	Finland	Chad	Ethiopia
Liechtenstein	France	China	Georgia
Luxembourg	Gabon	Congo, Dem. Rep.	Guyana
Maldives	Gambia	Costa Rica	Honduras
Malta	Germany	Cyprus	Iraq
Marshall Islands	Greece	Czech Republic	Kenya
Micronesia	Hong Kong (SAR)	Dominican Republic	Latvia
Monaco	Israel	El Salvador	Madagascar
Namibia	Italy	Equatorial Guinea	Malawi
Nauru	Japan	Ghana	Mauritania
New Zealand	Kuwait	Guatemala	Moldova
Niue	Lebanon	Haiti	Morocco
Oman	Libya	Hungary	Mozambique
Palau	Macau (SAR)	India	Nepal
Palestine	Mauritius	Indonesia	Nicaragua
Papua New Guinea	Netherlands	Iran	Sierra Leone
Paraguay	Norway	Kazakhstan	Slovenia
Saint Kitts and Nevis	Portugal	Kosovo	Somalia
Saint Lucia	Qatar	Kyrgyzstan	Tajikistan
Saint Vincent and the Grenadines	Rwanda	Laos	Zambia
Samoa	Saudi Arabia	Liberia	
San Marino	Singapore	Lithuania	

Continued

These economic, demographic, and labor market characteristics of host and source countries put international trafficking squarely in the context of the push and pull factors enumerated above. Doing so does not, however, allow one to distinguish the forces that govern international voluntary migration, for example, from the specific circumstances under which the trafficking of individuals occurs, including coercion, deceit, kidnapping, and forced or slave labor. To this end, we collected data on legislative and law enforcement variables in order to examine the extent to which international trafficking may also be looked at as a locational choice problem for criminal activities. These legislative and law enforcement variables are taken from the Protection Project (2002), the latest available years of the UN's *International Crime Victim Survey* and the *Seventh United Nations Survey of Crime Trends* of the United Nations (2004) for 2000.

Macroeconomic, Labor Market, and Demographic Factors

First, while systematic estimates of the size and scope of international trafficking are unavailable, our four-tier classification allows for a raw gauge of the share of the world's children who may be at risk of being trafficked. In particular, countries that are trafficking hubs host close to 77 percent of all children (ages 0–14) captured in our sample of 187 countries, yet these same countries account for only 18 percent of the total gross domestic product of all countries combined in 2000. An additional 9 percent of all children live in source countries of international trafficking, but these source countries produce 1 percent of the total gross domestic product of the 187 countries. The remaining 14 percent of children live in host countries (11.4 percent) and countries with no reported incidences of international trafficking (2.5 percent); combined, these two groups of countries account for over 81 percent of the total gross domestic product of the countries in our sample.

In terms of the labor force and demographic characteristics of these countries, a typical worker in a source country of international trafficking or a trafficking hub is more likely to be employed in agriculture as compared to a worker in a host country. We also observe a higher dependency ratio (ratio of children ages 0–14 to total population of a country) due primarily to the larger size of the child population in source countries and trafficking hubs. There is likewise a correspondingly higher incidence of child labor in source countries and trafficking hubs, with shares of economically active children (ages 10–14) 13.7 percent in source countries and 12.9 percent in trafficking hubs, compared to around 3.8 percent in host countries. Employment of adults, in contrast, exhibits the opposite pattern, with adult unemployment rates for both

TABLE 3.5
Global and Informational Links

	Host	Hub	Source	All
Trade Share of GDP (%)	86.32	77.11	87.35	87.06
International Tourism Expenditure (% imports)	6.42	4.91	6.02	5.77
International Tourism Receipt (% exports)	10.21	10.44	12.13	14.01
International Tourism Expenditure (% GDP)	2.84	1.94	2.79	2.66
International Tourism Receipt (% GDP)	5.55	3.69	3.65	6.57
Official Development Assistance (% GDP)	2.88	4.30	9.60	6.67

Indeed, international tourism receipts (whether as a fraction of export revenues or of gross national product) are on average smaller in countries that host trafficked victims in our sample.[5]

Legislations and Law Enforcement

There are a number of international conventions that are related to the condemnation of the trafficking of women and children. We have looked at the patterns of ratification of the ILO conventions on the Abolition of Forced Labour (105) and the Worst Forms of Child Labour (182), along with three other United Nations protocols: (i) calls for an end to the sale of children for the purposes of prostitution and pornography (OPSC), (ii) calls for an end to the trafficking of persons, especially women and children (PPSPT), and (iii) the Migrant Workers' Convention (MWC), which calls for the protection of the rights of migrant workers and members of their families.

As may be expected, the patterns of the ratification of these conventions differ widely (table 3.6). These patterns range from almost universal commitment to abolish forced labor, to the relative popularity, among host countries of trafficked individuals, of a commitment to eliminate the worst forms of child labor, which includes the sale of children and international trafficking. By contrast, ratification of the Migrant Workers Convention is more prevalent among source countries of international trafficking.

[5] Though beyond the scope of this chapter, global capital linkages between these four classes and the rest of the world exhibit a rather more systematic pattern. For example, source countries of international trafficking and trafficking hubs are more dependent on official development assistance than are host countries of international trafficking.

TABLE 3.7
Crime and Law Enforcement

	Host	Hub	Source	All
Police Personnel (per 100K)	289.65	288.78	272.04	286.38
Total Recorded Crimes (per 100K)	4918.92	1825.94	1387.27	2991.97
Total Convicted Persons (per 100K)	809.62	735.15	337.01	692.38
Convicted Persons per Recorded Crime	0.17	0.30	0.41	0.27
Rule of Law Index	0.73	−0.30	−0.52	0.01

In addition to the enactment of national laws and the ratification of international conventions, one might argue that of even more importance is the extent to which these laws are enforced. To this end, table 3.7 summarizes data taken from the UN *Survey of Crime Trends (Seventh Survey)* for 2000. The capacity of policy enforcement is expressed in two ways. The variable *police* denotes the number of police personnel per 100 thousand persons. The variable *convicted persons per crime* gives the number of convicted persons per reported crime in a country. The variable *police* allows us to pin down the physical capacity of the police force, while, the variable *convicted persons per crime* is concerned with the efficiency of the police force. These two variables give two very different pictures of the capability of police enforcements. In particular, host countries have, on average, a higher police force per capita than do source countries and trafficking hubs. Nevertheless, the number of convicted persons per recorded crime is also the lowest there.

These conflicting observations may have to do with underreporting in official police data. There are two reasons why underreporting in source countries is of interest in the context of trafficking. First, for traffickers operating in potential source countries, underreporting is of course advantageous, since the likelihood of getting caught is accordingly lower. Second, underreporting may also be a signal of the public's distrust of the police force, due for instance to corruption among public officials. Both of these factors concern the degree of access to effective law enforcement, and separate the (economic) push and pull factors of international migration, as distinct from the criminal activities associated with international trafficking.[7] As a partial remedy to this issue of access, we will further make use of the "rule of law" governance indicator[8] from Kaufmann, Kraay, and Zoido-Lobaton (1999a, 1999b).

---

[7] Exactly why report rates are lower in source countries is of course of independent interest, although it is certainly beyond the scope of this chapter.

[8] The "rule of law" indicator is a composite index of (i) voice (e.g., freedom of press and freedom to associate) and accountability; (ii) political and stability/lack of violence;

TABLE 3.8
Gravity Model of the Push and Pull Factors of Trafficking Basic Economic and
Geographic Variables

		Dependent Variable: Incidence of Trafficking of Women and Children		
		I	II	III
Host Country	lrgdppc	0.625***	0.703***	0.625***
		0.030	0.145	0.031
	transition	−1.286***	−2.176***	−1.201***
		0.208	0.901	0.210
	gini		−0.008	
			0.020	
	landlock			−0.443***
				0.140
Source Country	lrgdppc	−0.431***	−0.953***	−0.511***
		0.028	0.201	0.032
	transition	1.756***	3.474***	1.984***
		0.112	0.603	0.116
	gini		0.107***	
			0.025	
	landlock			−0.649***
				0.109
Common	constant	−6.943***	−7.673***	−6.235***
		0.321	2.393	0.351
	Region (comreg)	yes***	yes***	yes***
	Border (comborder)	yes***	yes***	yes***
N		28056	870	28056
Wald Chi²		964.680	81.830	950.780
Prob > Chi²		0.000	0.000	0.000
Pseudo R²		0.206	0.339	0.215
Log Likelihood		−2154.613	−111.172	−2131.545

  * Significant at 1% level.
  ** Significant at 5% level.
  *** Significant at 10% level.

check whether income inequality within countries (as opposed to income inequality across countries) has a role to play in raising the likelihood of trafficking, reduces the number of available observations by a great deal. However, the results are in support of Rogers and Swinnerton (2001), and

10 percent of the population has access to 10 percent of national income), while a value of 1 indicates perfect inequality in the distribution of income (for example, the top 1 percent of the population has access to all or 100 percent of national income).

		(1)	(2)	(3)	(4)	(5)
	iloc182	0.269***	0.347***	0.353***		
		0.104	0.101	0.098		
	ppspt	0.377***	0.370***		0.374***	
		0.099	0.098		0.098	
	opsc	−0.045	−0.099			−0.109
		0.142	0.139			0.138
	transition	yes***	yes***	yes***	yes***	yes***
	landlock	yes***	yes***	yes***	yes***	yes***
Common	constant	−5.640***	−5.332***	−6.162***	−6.237***	−6.011***
		0.398	0.392	0.356	0.357	0.360
	Region	yes***	yes***	yes***	yes***	yes***
	Border	yes***	yes***	yes***	yes***	yes***
N		23256	23562	23562	23562	23562
Wald Chi²		1014.860	993.920	877.580	904.350	904.350
Prob > Chi²		0.000	0.000	0.000	0.000	0.000
Pseudo R²		0.238	0.235	0.216	0.215	0.212
Log Likelihood		1875.809	1886.411	1933.292	−1937.685	1944.462

* Significant at 1% level.
** Significant at 5% level.
*** Significant at 10% level.

prostitution	0.245	0.245	0.352	0.306	0.364
	0.303***	0.284***	0.380	0.507**	0.237
	0.092	0.091	0.247	0.218	0.251
rule of law		-0.282**			-1.410***
		0.084			0.254
report rate	-0.023***		-0.097***		
	0.008		0.021		
police				0.001	
				0.001	
conviction rate			-1.049***		-1.213***
			0.447		0.441
transition	yes***	yes***	yes***	yes***	yes***
landlock	yes***	yes***	yes*	yes	yes*
Common constant	-4.919***	-6.066***	-1.903***	-4.960***	-6.067***
	0.385	0.645	1.445	1.282	2.115
Region	yes***	yes***	yes***	yes***	yes***
Border	yes***	yes***	yes***	yes***	yes***
N	22052	22052	2352	2756	2352
Wald Chi²	920.410	909.790	199.200	236.980	203.330
Prob > Chi²	0.000	0.000	0.000	0.000	0.000
Pseudo R²	0.232	0.231	0.310	0.257	0.316
Log Likelihood	1949.345	1950.047	375.502	387.105	372.689

* Significant at 1% level.
** Significant at 5% level.
*** Significant at 10% level.

(2004), our results indicate that the provision of amnesty and the inflow of trafficked victims appear to go hand in hand. Meanwhile, the banning of prostitution and the outflow of trafficked victims also appear to be positively correlated.

Although these latter empirical findings might seem counterintuitive, there is a logical explanation to these observed outcomes. In a series of theoretical papers (Basu and Chau 2005; Basu and Seiberg 2005), we find that these paradoxical results may be due to the impact that legislations have on the push and pull factors of trafficking, and on the incentives for traffickers. First, the granting of asylum in host countries reduces the number of trafficked prostitutes. However, if the demand for services rendered by prostitutes remains unchanged, then the returns to prostitution will rise with the granting of asylum in the countries. Subsequently, it becomes more lucrative for traffickers to target countries that grant asylum to trafficked individuals as potential destinations.

On the other hand, a ban on prostitution in the source countries either reduces the supply of prostitutes or raises the price commanded by those involved in the sex trade. Both these factors raise the opportunity income of traffickers. Instead of taking an individual out of a country, traffickers have the alternative to engage the individual in illegal prostitution within the source country. The increased profits from this illegal prostitution strengthen the bargaining power of traffickers abroad, as they can now negotiate a better price for those taken to the host country. In sum, the twin objectives of granting legal rights to trafficked individuals and reducing the incidence of trafficking conflict, unless (i) adequate attention is paid to the perverse incentives of traffickers and (ii) greater efficiency is attained in the apprehension of traffickers in host and source countries.

Child Labor in Debt Bondage

Debt bondage is generally defined as the pledge by a debtor of his personal services and/or the services of people under his control as repayment of monetary loans. The adoption of the ILO convention on the Worst Forms of Child Labour represented one among myriad international actions that target child labor resulting from debt bondage. Notable amongst these are (i) law enforcement efforts such as the training of labor inspectors to enforce child labor laws (ILO-IPEC 1997); (ii) direct action assisting and providing funding for governments and local NGOs to liberate children from debt bondage and to provide education, small business loans, and other forms of assistance (InFocus Programme 2002); and (iii) extranational initiatives that condition international trade benefits upon the extent of child labor and bonded labor practices.

labor services (adult and child) pledged to the landlord in the peak season. This leads to a low labor demand in the peak season, which keeps the market wage down, preventing individuals from saving and forcing them to engage in debt bondage the next lean season.

A careful look at the forces that perpetuate debt bondage underscores an important institutional failure—the lack of savings for poor individuals, which increases the likelihood of exposure to consumption shortfalls in the lean season, when income is uncertain. In this respect, if individuals could either bargain for a better credit-labor contract or negotiate through a labor union higher wages in the peak season, then debt bondage would be a far less pervasive phenomenon. Therefore, we start by looking at the national legislations currently in place in India, Nepal, and Pakistan that provides individuals in rural households the right to negotiate for better wages.

India   The Bonded Labor System (Abolition) Act of 1976 prohibits all forms of bonded labor. However, debt bondage continues to be prevalent in rural India, particularly in the states of Bihar, Orissa, and Andhra Pradesh (U.S. Department of Labor 1995). Bonded child laborers are reportedly pledged to employers by parents typically in exchange for a loan (U.S. Department of Labor 1995). In a 1979 survey carried out in ten states of India, about 30 percent of families under debt bondage put one or more children into bondage, mostly to cover debt repayment. The situation is compounded by the lack of bargaining power on the part of agricultural workers in the rural areas of India. Indeed, legal protections of worker rights are effective only for the 28 million workers in the organized industrial sector, out of a total workforce of more than 397.2 million (Bureau of Democracy, Human Rights and Labor 1999; Tucker 1996).

Nepal   Bonded labor is a continuing problem in agriculture in Nepal, even though the Nepal Labor Act specifically prohibits forced or bonded child labor (Bureau of Democracy, Human Rights and Labor 1999). An estimated 100,000 individuals work under the bonded labor system in the southern Terai region. In many cases, the entire family, including children, is involved in performing the tasks required, and bondage with the landlord is expected to terminate only when debt is paid off in full. Like India, legal protection that provides for the freedom of association and the right to unionize is, in practice, limited to those employed in the formal sector of the economy. Collective bargaining agreements cover an estimated 20 percent of wage earners in the organized sector (Bureau of Democracy, Human Rights and Labor 1999).

Pakistan   The use of slaves and forced labor is outlawed in Pakistan by the Constitution of 1973 (article 11). Meanwhile, the Bonded Labor System (Abolition) Act adopted in 1992 outlawed bonded labor, canceled existing bonded debts, and forbade lawsuits for the recovery of existing debts (Bureau of Democracy, Human Rights and Labor 1999). Despite

TABLE 3.11
Government and NGO Statistics on Debt Bondage in India, Nepal and Pakistan

Country	Participation Rates (ages 5–14)	% of Rural Population	Legislations Outlawing Bondage	Survey	Incidence of Bondage	Collective Bargaining
India	5.57% (11.5 million)	71.50%	Yes	Government of India (1979) Tucker (1996)	353,000* 2.6–15 million	Industrial 28 million out of estimated 397.2 million
Nepal	26.5% (1.55 million)	80.50%	Yes	ISSC (1992)	100,000**	20% of organized sector
Pakistan	14.7% (3.3 million)	75%	Yes	Kamiya System Human Rights Commission of Pakistan	2 million***	Industrial workers only

* 30% of families put one or more children to work in order to repay debt.
** Incidence of bonded child labor is higher for landless households. In 46% of the cases, there is more than one child working for a wage.
*** Bonded child labor is extensively used in sugar cane and cotton farms.

These capture, though imperfectly, the observed "price" and "quantity" of access to credit market. An additional variable *bankfin* is taken from the Heritage index of banking and finance (1995–99 average). This is a five-point score indicating decreasing degrees of freedom of the private sector to access banking and financial services.

In order to measure the degree of access to consumption-smoothing loans, whether from formal or informal sources, we constructed an indicator *riskshare*. This is obtained by estimating the extent to which variability in gross domestic product per capita ($\Delta \log y_{it}$) translates to a corresponding variability of household consumption per capita ($\Delta \log c_{it}$) (1970–98, constant 1995 prices). Data on gross domestic product and household consumption per capita are taken from World Bank (2001). For each country *i*, the variable *riskshare* is taken to be the estimated least squares regression coefficient β_i of the following regression equation:

$$\Delta \log c_{it} = \alpha_i + \beta_i \Delta \log y_{it} + \varepsilon_{it}$$

If $\beta_i = 0$, the household consumption is fully insured from per capita income shocks. At the other extreme, with $\beta_i = 1$, there is perfect pass-through of income variability to household consumption variability.

In all, child labor in debt bondage is reported in 43 of the 134 countries for which data are available. As may be expected, child labor in debt bondage is a developing country phenomenon, although the converse is not true (table 3.13). Approximately 60 percent of countries free from observed incidence of debt bondage are in fact low- and middle-income countries (World Bank 2001). In addition, the per capita GDP (1994–98) level of $4489 perfectly separates the two groups of countries, those with and without bondage. As in Krueger (1997), there is likewise a threshold income level dividing countries with and without child labor.

Indeed, over 40 percent of countries with reported incidence of children in debt bondage are exporters of non-fuel primary products, with agricultural exports contributing to more than 50 percent of total export revenue. Despite this apparent dependence on agriculture, the value added of agricultural workers is significantly lower in countries where debt bondage exists.

In terms of the adoption of core labor standards in the two groups of countries, the average percentage of economically active children (10–14 years of age) is about 23 times higher in countries where children in debt bondage is reported (table 3.14). This is despite the fact that almost all of the countries included in the dataset have adopted international conventions or national legislation on minimum worker age in one form or another. The rights for workers to negotiate wages and form unions are much more popularly observed in countries in which children in debt bondage are not at issue. Surprisingly, legislative exceptions for child labor

TABLE 3.14
Observance of Core Labor Standards and Financial Indicators

	bondchild = 0					bondchild = 1				
	Mean	Std. Dev.	Min	Max	Obs	Mean	Std. Dev.	Min	Max	Obs
Observance of Labor Rights										
Child Labor (% of children 10–14)	1.465	5.782	0	37.93	80	23.22	13.82	0.1	52.67	43
legexag	0.66	0.479	0	1	50	0.733	0.45	0	1	30
enforce	3.405	0.964	1	4	42	2.214	0.579	1	3	14
Financial Sector Development Indicators										
Intspread (%)	8.962	12.12	1.203	75.16	53	10.29	7.392	3.026	30.78	21
riskshare	0.823	0.605	-1.039	3.422	67	0.926	0.283	0.36	1.768	32
bankfin	2.819	1.018	1	5	78	3.364	0.838	2	5	39
priv (%)	59.47	33.6	9.438	166.2	35	21.62	16.7	2.766	74.4	18

TABLE 3.15
Logit Regression (Debt Bondage)
Stage of Development, Core Labor Rights and Financial Development

	Dependent Variable: Incidence of Child Labor Due to Debt Bondage			
	I	*II*	*III*	*IV*
lrgdppc	−1.9388***	−2.0658***	−2.2702***	−2.0426***
	(−2.46)	(−3.46)	(−2.19)	(−3.84)
intspread	0.1663			
	(0.275)			
bankfin		−1.1137		
		(−0.116)		
priv			2.3703	
			(0.55)	
riskshare				3.3389*
				(1.79)
enforce	−1.7213***	−0.6750	−0.6355	−0.0543
	(−2.48)	(−1.43)	(−0.79)	(−0.07)
constant	17.5038***	20.1275***	17.1691***	12.8437***
	(2.54)	(3.08)	(2.98)	(3.98)
N	40	55	41	50
Wald Chi^2	12.1900	16.6900	16.5900	18.9200
Prob > Chi^2	0.0068	0.0008	0.0009	0.0003
Pseudo R^2	0.7045	0.5937	0.6408	0.6049
Log Likelihood	−6.3026	−12.6779	−7.7504	−11.7130

  * Significant at 1% level.
  ** Significant at 5% level.
  *** Significant at 10% level.

Moreover, a stricter enforcement of legislation concerning debt bondage can simply encourage poor individuals to send their children into other (possibly worse) forms of work to generate income for the household. Similarly, cheaper access to formal credit for households reduces the incidence of debt bondage. However, easier access to credit also leaves open the possibility of households overborrowing and then sending their children to work in order to repay their loans. Both these forms of intervention reduce the vulnerability of households to engage in debt bondage but may be unsuccessful in preventing the incidence of child labor *per se*. Two policies that seem to have a positive effect on eliminating both child labor in debt bondage, and child labor in general, are (i) the enforcement of the right to unionize and collectively bargain for higher wages and (ii) the institution of rural public works programs. For example, the rural public

and targeted towards accomplishing the twin objectives of granting human rights to those enslaved and reducing the incidence of these two problems. However, the issue of the worst forms of child labor, particularly child slavery in the two above forms, has received very little attention from economic theorists and empiricists. As we have argued, systematic cross-country analysis underscores the problems inherent in achieving the twin objectives stated above, simply because there are multiple market imperfections associated with the emergence of these two forms of slavery. Instead of granting asylum to trafficked victims, effective policy intervention entails stricter enforcement of trafficking laws and heavier punishments for those involved in trafficking, simultaneously in the host and source countries. In the case of debt bondage, instead of redeeming children by repaying their outstanding debts, a far more effective policy would be to institute rural public works programs during the lean season and enforce the right to unionize and collectively bargain for wages.

Bibliography

Baland, J. M., and James Robinson (2000), "Is Child Labor Inefficient?" *Journal of Political Economy* 108: 663–679.

Basu, Arnab K. (2002), "Oligopsonistic Landlords, Segmented Labor Markets and the Persistence of Tied-Labor Contracts," *American Journal of Agricultural Economics* 84: 438–53.

Basu, Arnab K., and Nancy H. Chau (2003), "Targeting Child Labor in Debt Bondage: Evidence Theory and Policy Prescriptions," *World Bank Economic Review* 17: 255–281.

Basu, Arnab K., and Nancy H. Chau (2004), "Exploitation of Child Labor and the Dynamics of Debt Bondage"; *Journal of Economic Growth* 9: 209–238.

Basu, Arnab K., and Nancy H. Chau (2005), "Trafficking in Women and Children as a Locational Choice: Theory and Evidence." Unpublished paper, Department of Economics, College of William and Mary, Williamsburg, VA.

Basu, Arnab K., and Katri Seiberg (2005), "A Simple Model of Child Prostitution and Trafficking." Unpublished paper, Department of Economics, College of William and Mary, Williamsburg, VA.

Basu, Kaushik, and Pham Hoang Van (1998), "The Economics of Child Labor," *American Economic Review* 88: 412–427.

Beck, Thorsten, Asli Demirguc-Kunt, and Ross Levine (2000), "A New Database on Financial Development and Structure," *World Bank Economic Review*, September: 597–605.

Becker, Gary (1968), "Crime and Punishment: An Economic Approach," *Journal of Political Economy* 76: 169–217.

Brenton, Paul (2000), "Globalisation and Social Exclusion in the EU: Policy Implications." Center for European Policy Studies, Brussels, working document no. 159.

Future—A Synthesis Report. Geneva: International Labor Organization, *http://www.ilo.org/public/english/standards/ipec/publ/policy/synrep97/*.

Kanbur, Ravi (2003), "On Noxious Markets," in P. Pattanaik and S. Cullenberg (eds.), *Globalization, Culture and the Limits of the Market: New Essays in Economics and Philosophy*, (New Delhi: Oxford University Press).

Karim, Farhad (1995), *Contemporary Forms of Slavery in Pakistan*. New York: Human Rights Watch.

Kaufmann, Daniel, Aart Kraay., and Pablo Zoido-Lobaton (1999a), "Aggregating Governance Indicators," *World Bank Policy Research Department Working Paper* no. 2195.

Kaufmann, Daniel, Aart Kraay., and Pablo Zoido-Lobaton (1999b), "Governance Matters," *World Bank Policy Research Department* working paper no. 2196.

Krueger, Alan (1997), "International Labor Standards and Trade," in Michael Bruno and Boris Pleskovic (eds.), *Annual World Bank Conference on Development Economics, 1996* (Washington, DC: The World Bank).

Levitt, S. D. (1997), "Using Electoral Cycles in Police Hiring to Estimate the Effect of Police on Crime," *American Economic Review* 87: 270–290.

Lipsey R. G., and Lancaster K. (1956), "The General Theory of the Second-Best," *Review of Economic Studies* 24: 11–32.

Office of the United States Trade Representative (1997), "Monitoring and Enforcing Trade Laws and Agreements—Fact Sheet." Washington, DC: Office of the United States Trade Representative, Executive Office of the President, September 30.

Organization for Economic Cooperation and Development (OECD) (2000), "International Trade and Core Labor Standards." Paris: Directorate for Employment Labor and Social Affairs, OECD.

Protection Project (2002), *Human Rights Report on Trafficking in Persons, Especially Women and Children*. Baltimore: John Hopkins University.

Ranjan, P. (1999), "An Economic Analysis of Child Labor," *Economics Letters* 64: 99–105.

Ranjan, P. (2001), "Credit Constraints and the Phenomenon of Child Labor," *Journal of Development Economics* 64: 81–102.

Rogers, C., and Kenneth Swinnerton (2001), "Inequality, Productivity, and Child Labor: Theory and Evidence." Working Paper, Georgetown University, Department of Economics, Washington, DC.

Rogers, C., and Kenneth Swinnerton (2002), "A Theory of Exploitative Child Labor," Working Paper, Washington, DC: United States Department of Labor.

Satz, Debra (2003a), "Noxious Markets: Why Some Things Should Not Be for Sale," in P. Pattanaik and S. Cullenberg (eds.), *Globalization, Culture and the Limits of the Market: New Essays in Economics and Philosophy* (New Delhi: Oxford University Press).

Satz, Debra (2003b), "Child Labor: A Normative Perspective," *World Bank Economic Review* 17: 297–309.

Soares, Rodrigo (2004), "Development, Crime and Punishment: Accounting for the International Differences in Crime Rates," *Journal of Development Economics* 73: 155–184.

Stigler, George (1970), "The Optimum Enforcement of Laws," *Journal of Political Economy* 78: 526–536.

Chapter Four

Slavery, Freedom, and Sen

STANLEY ENGERMAN

Introduction

Economic historians have long wrestled with the tensions between useful and measurable economic perspectives on changes in welfare associated with development, such as that denoted by the standard of living, and a broader, less tangible, approach summarized as the quality of life.[1] In *Development as Freedom*, Amartya Sen summarizes his recent thinking on the meaning of development, returning with new insight to this tension in evaluating economic changes.

Sen has long rejected more conventional economic interpretations of the standard of living in terms of opulence based solely on material conditions and suggested instead an interpretation in terms of people's capabilities and functionings. Functionings are the various things that a person may value doing or being. For example, not being enslaved is a valuable functioning, just as is living a life of normal length (or longer) or being healthy. A person's capability refers to the feasible set or sets of functionings that circumstances allow him or her to achieve.[2] As Amartya Sen (1999, 75) says, "capability is thus a kind of freedom: the substantive freedom to achieve alternative functioning combinations (or less formally put, the freedom to achieve various lifestyles)."[3] When the

---

Chapter 4 (excluding the addendum) originally appeared (in a longer form) in *Feminist Economics* 9 (2–3), 2003: 185–211 (http://www.journalsonline.tandf.co.uk/openurl.asp?genre=article&issn=1354-5701&volume=9&issue=2&spage=185) and is reprinted here with permission of Taylor & Francis Ltd and the Journals Association (The International Association for Feminist Economics).

[1] For a survey of the earlier debate on the British standard of living in the Industrial Revolution and some proposed expansions of the concept, see Engerman (1994).

[2] See, for earlier discussions of these concepts, Amartya Sen (1980, 1993).

[3] Sen (1999, 87–110) points to certain important deprivations of individual capacities related to, but not conceptually the same as, low incomes, premature mortality, undernourishment, persistent morbidity, widespread illiteracy, and missing women. All but the last

occurrence in human societies, generally reflecting dire circumstances faced by persons at the lowest income levels. Even in discussing Sen's "goods," trade-offs exist regarding costs, resources, and expenditure allocations. This paper shows that for people living at the level of subsistence, important trade-offs are made between different basic capabilities. The paper is located empirically in the context of slavery, a context which Sen himself has explored. The literature on slavery shows that, at times, people have been forced to make trade-offs between basic capabilities. Slavery, therefore, is sometimes the outcome of people having to make choices between different aspects of freedom, such as between the freedom to be liberated and live free and the freedom to survive and be healthy.

Sen's conceptualization of freedom in terms of expanding capabilities has to confront the issue that people, past and present, have had to make trade-offs between different basic freedoms or capabilities. Examining slavery can give us some insights into the dynamics of those trade-offs. Finally, and again consistent with Sen's interests, this paper discusses a gender perspective on the nature of the trade-offs explored. The freedoms of male and female slaves were violated and curbed in different ways and to different extents, and the nature of new freedoms and the choices that followed emancipation were likewise gendered. This paper emphasizes the harsh trade-offs between freedoms that slaves faced and suggests that they are echoed in the bitter choices that continue to confront many disadvantaged peoples today, especially women and children.

Slavery and Freedom

Slavery has taken many different forms; it has been among the most frequent of human institutions, existing in almost all societies in the past and in most parts of the world. Slaves have experienced different work regimes and differences in physical and material treatment, depending on various economic, political, cultural, and ideological circumstances. Nevertheless, the coercion permitted slaveowners has been almost universal, with the limitations on choices permitted to slaves who have always been subject to the master's control. Lost liberties have often been the outcome of involuntary acts; however, in societies with low and/or highly variable levels of income, people have been willing to sacrifice their liberties and those of their family members in exchange for the ability to survive.

At the lowest levels of income, where slavery became a preferred alternative to weakness or death, the conditions of the free were often similarly dire, and moving out of slavery did not mean any material benefits to the newly freed. "Voluntary" slavery has a long and geographically dispersed history, but there is only very limited literature on the topic. Societies with voluntary slavery, as all poor societies, seem to have lacked

of the high material standard of living of U.S. slaves to contrast the value of freedom with the judgments made from "an evaluative system that focuses only on culmination outcomes" (Sen 1999, 28, citing Fogel and Engerman 1974). Freedom implies the ability to make choices, which may include earning less in return for more leisure, less intensity of work, more time with family, more desired geographic location, and so on.[6] From this perspective it appears clear that measured income is not to be regarded as an accurate measure of welfare if the achievement of high levels of material consumption is at the cost of actions that can limit individual and family choice. Several questions may be raised about Sen's argument on this point. Freedom is not easy to define, since it may relate to individual rights or to group freedoms. Even what many consider to be freedom (in contrast with slavery) includes a number of legal and social constraints which, while perhaps less limiting than systems based on absolute government fiat, mean that individuals do not have unlimited choice or are not always treated equally.

Choices and Freedom

All people make choices from among available opportunities but under constraints, whether imposed by nature, by other people, or by the self. This choice process is examined in the basic economic model of consumer behavior. Individuals do not all choose the same alternative, reflecting differences in tastes, differences in incomes, and differences in the nature of the constraints faced. Changing constraints with unchanged tastes will generally lead to the selection of different alternatives, as will changing tastes with unchanged constraints. The constraints may be natural, as in the Malthusian limit on the capacity of land to provide adequate food, or they may be social, either deriving from the power of certain groups or individuals or else by some apparently agreed-upon set of enforced codes, legal or otherwise. The market imposes constraints even though people may be legally free to make choices, as long as prices and incomes limit opportunities (Hale 1952; Steinfeld 2001).[7] The more limiting the constraints and the fewer the alternatives available, the less free

---

[6] The dilemma was, of course, well known, and goes back a very long time. The Greek atomist Democritus wrote, apparently some time in the middle of the fifth century BC, "poverty in a democracy is preferable to so-called prosperity among dictators to the same extent as freedom is to slavery." On the gender issue, Democritus claimed (as have many others in later years) that "some men rule cities but are slaves to women." See Paul Cartledge (1998, 35, 38).

[7] For a comparison of labor coercion under slavery and freedom, see O. Nigel Bolland (2002).

coercive relationships which are intended to restrict choice, if presumably for the benefit of the coerced. The distinctions drawn between the choices open for men and for women suggest a similar lack of equality and the relative absence of a decision-making capability granted women. The difficulties of defining freedoms within a social group or a family group still remain, as illustrated by recent debates on such issues as the acceptability of the long-time practice of female genital mutilation in some cultures, defining of the rights of children, and the ability of women to re-define the terms of the marriage contract.

Gender, age, and legal status define some of the groups that have confronted limitations on their freedoms. Children are traditionally treated as incapable of making rational choices up to some specified age (the age itself being a major source of disagreement) at which time they become adults able to make their own choices. Women were long regarded as not fully capable of making choices, which accounted for their special treatment in legislation, a condition that still exits in many places. This sometimes meant their being given more favorable treatment than men, although this often meant limitations on their rights to freely choose living and working conditions. Similar types of controls, limiting freedom of action, have been applied to the aged, the mentally disabled, the physically disabled, and convicts and felons, among other groups.[10] The most extreme case of constraints on personal freedom is slavery.

Slavery, Freedom, and Living Conditions

The complexities of contrasting slavery and freedom often arise from the expectation that "all good things go together," and that freedom necessarily entails better living conditions and more rapid economic growth than does slavery. Sen (1999, 29) notes that while it is possible that slaves in the United State did have higher material living standards than did free workers, nevertheless "slaves did run away, and there were excellent reasons for presuming that the interests of the slaves were not well served by the system of slavery." Nevertheless, the low rate of runaways in most slave societies suggests that various means of maintaining the system were used, including force as well as rewards, in the short and long run. The desire to avoid enslavement seems obvious, and the flight of southern U.S. slaves when northern armies moved into the South was not surprising, but under customary conditions in the U.S. South, as in

[10] Debates, similar for all these groups, relate to the questions of whether appropriate policies to offset inequality are affirmative action programs, cash grants, or provision of more education, and also concerning the trade-off between short-run and long-run benefits.

without the protection of a "trusted white man" the ex-slaves were fearful of kidnapping or violence.[12]

Recent studies of slave societies have shown that slave economies were capable of experiencing rapid economic growth using a production system of gang labor and had an ability to adjust to changes in world demand for export commodities by changing crop patterns and geographic locations to achieve growth (Fogel 1989, 17–113). It has also been shown that some slaves were provided with consumption levels in excess of those of some members of the free populations in the same country and, as was the case for U.S. slaves, of most populations elsewhere in the world (Fogel 1989, 132–47). Such higher standards of living may have reflected the master's perceptions of what was needed to secure a greater intensity of work. That skilled slaves were granted higher material compensation while their prices were above those of other slaves indicates that the returns to skilled human capital were divided in some uncertain proportion between slaves and masters. In many cases there was a surplus above subsistence to be fought over, and negotiated divisions between masters and slaves were the outcome. There is a difference, in some important regards, between legal status and economic status. Slaveowners did not always do what they were legally permitted to do (which included rather complete control over the slave's life and body), although at times they exceeded their rights.

Manumissions and Emancipations

The process of manumission provided individual slaves with freedom and gave them certain other rights (but not always all those granted citizens), yet without affecting the status of those still enslaved. Newcomers to a nation or newly freed ex-slaves would not be given the full set of rights that belong to the "established" members of society. Those considered, for whatever reasons, to be outsiders lack key rights and therefore suffer limitations in their freedom. In some cases, freedom can be regarded as a zero-sum game, gains for some coming only at the expense of others, so that measures to increase the freedom of everyone are not possible. While freedom refers to self-ownership by individuals, legal and other constraints may limit the choices open to nominally free individuals.

[12] See Ulrich Phillips (1909, II, 161–164; 1918, 446–447); Kenneth Stampp (1956, 92–93); Eugene Genovese (1974, 399–401); Deborah White (1985, 117–118); and Orlando Patterson (1982, 27).

The legacy of the past was present, but the availability of new opportunities permitted different outcomes even if some things, such as the allocation of land ownership, did not often change (Engerman 2000).[14]

A general pattern in most New World slave emancipations was the decline of the plantation system.[15] The desire of ex-slaves was to move to smaller agricultural units, whether owned, rented, or labored on, resembling in size and structure the farms of those yeomen who had always been free. These, however, were often less productive than were the plantations, so that the end of slavery usually meant a decline in output, and in some cases it took societies several decades to reach the level of per capita output achieved under slavery. The archetypical case here was Haiti, where emancipation, despite some attempts of the new rulers to bring back a sugar plantation system, ultimately meant the development of an economy based on small farms, producing primarily foodstuff for local markets and with a substantial decline in labor productivity. Wherever small farms replaced plantations, the economic benefits of gang labor were lost. Haiti, once possibly the world's richest area, today has a measured level of per capita output possibly below the level at the end of the eighteenth century, and is the one country in the western hemisphere to have an income at sub-Saharan levels.[16] Ironically, given the successful end of the plantation system, in the twentieth century Haitian migrants produced sugar on plantations in the Dominican Republic and Cuba.

There were exceptions to this general pattern, reflecting differences in natural or political constraints in different areas. On Barbados and Antigua, for example, the population density was so high that ex-slaves had nowhere to go and remained on the plantations at least until their external migration increased in the late nineteenth century. In areas such as Trinidad, Jamaica, and British Guiana, the aims of British colonial policy were initially the same, since there were large expanses of unsettled land. Although many of the ex-slaves were able to leave the plantations and establish small farms in the interior, not all were able to do so. In those areas where sugar cultivation remained highly productive, such as Trinidad and British Guiana, the plantation system was restored within

[14] The one area with a dramatic change in land ownership patterns was Haiti, where the slaves freed themselves in a revolt and drove out their former owners.

[15] Exceptions, in the British Caribbean, were Barbados and Antigua, where land shortages meant the workers had limited opportunities, and Trinidad and British Guiana, which attracted indentured laborers to work on their plantations. Later Cuba attracted immigrants to help maintain the plantation system.

[16] Haiti's initial difficulties were due, in part, to external interferences, such as the lack of desire on the part of most countries to trade with it, and a need to pay, after the 1820s, an indemnity to France in exchange for the opening of trade. Moreover, Haiti has long been politically and economically unstable.

greater degrees of occupational divergence between black men and black women than had existed under slavery, as discussed below.

The ending of slavery and the freeing of the labor force had a substantial impact in reducing overall output, particularly the output of plantation export crops, in most societies formerly based on slavery. Where it has been possible to prepare estimates, it has been shown that were declines in per capita income of significant magnitudes for several decades. Thus the free labor argument of higher outputs anticipated in the aftermath of slavery argued for by many did not occur quickly, and in several cases it required the importation either of contract labor from India and China or of free European labor from Spain or Italy.

What is more difficult to analyze is the effect of emancipation on the consumption level of ex-slaves to determine this aspect of the benefits of emancipation beyond freedom. While the initial changes may not have led to dramatically higher income, freedom permitted the ex-slaves to reap benefits from increased productivity in future years.[17] In the U.S. South the first decades of freedom did see increased mortality for ex-slaves, and there was an overall decline in southern production of foodstuffs. In the West Indies there were declines in food imports, suggesting a lessened availability of foodstuffs there. The estimates of food consumption needed to firmly establish the impact of emancipation upon living standards are still not conclusive, but declines in the initial years would not be implausible given estimates of overall production, and the important fact that redistribution of land ownership did not generally take place, so that some return to landowners continued. Whatever redistribution did occur did not mean that ex-slaves would gain their entire product after the end of slavery.

In most places the gang system no longer existed after slavery, and it is probable that the hours and/or intensity of labor fell with freedom. However, even as freedom broadened the options for mobility and labor choice among ex-slaves, the pattern of the U.S. South, where life expectation declined for several decades, food consumption in rural areas was probably lowered, and dietary diseases became more frequent, suggests significant negative material effects. The relative impacts on males and females of the changing life expectation and magnitudes of consumption are not clear, but the nature of living arrangements and provision of consumption goods did change dramatically with the move from plantations and white-owned small units to small farms operated by blacks.

[17] Food for slaves could be obtained either by master purchase and provision or by the slaves growing their own food on master-provided plots of land. For a discussion of food provisioning in the British West Indies, see B. W. Higman (1984, 204–218). Under the system of master provision, by purchase, of foodstuffs, females spent more time in field labor and therefore presumably learnt less about small-scale production of foodstuffs.

probably some decline in the percentage of black females married, an increase in the age of first birth, and an increase in the number of black childless women (Engerman 1983). Whether this reflected an increased control of birth and marriage patterns by black females or, as has been argued, an increase in diseases is not clear, but for United States blacks the end of slavery meant declining fertility, whereas in other parts of the Americas there may have initially been some increased fertility after emancipation (see, e.g., Roberts 1957, 216–72; Higman 1984, 347–73).

In the U.S. South, as elsewhere where slave emancipation occurred, there were significant changes in family arrangements and gender relations resulting from the shift from plantations of several families to residence on small farms operated by individual families.[20] There were declines in fertility after emancipation, in part because of the increase in the free family's costs of raising children to adulthood with the ending of the plantation's collective child-care arrangement and also the loss of the implicit subsidy to child-raising costs made by plantation owners. In most slave societies females had been valued at about 80 to 90 percent of same-aged males in the same work category, although until age 15 females were equal in price to males (Moreno Fraginals, Klein, and Engerman 1983). The wage differentials by sex among freed people were often larger than the price and hiring rate differentials had been under slavery. Much of the domestic work, such as food preparation and cleaning, had been undertaken during slavery by a limited number of specialized slaves, and a large portion of slave females specialized in field work. After emancipation household work was done in one-family households by women allocating their time among several different functions. Black women now had work patterns that, for whatever reason, resembled those of white females, particularly those of the working class. They spent more time outside the labor force, working in the home, and less in the field than when enslaved, and female wage earners most frequently worked as domestic servants.

After emancipation in the United States South, ex-slave families frequently followed the pattern of two-parent households (whether coresident or in separate residence) which had existed under slavery, a pattern which was to change dramatically in the last half of the twentieth century, when the proportion of female-headed households, particularly in urban areas, increased. Whatever the explanation for this recent rise in the proportion of black female-headed households, it is of interest

---

[20] The precise effects on fertility of the antebellum pattern of some slave couples living on different farms, or with separate residences, were, however, unclear. Under slavery, particularly in Virginia, there were cross-unit marriages with visiting, etc. Yet the areas in which these occurred seem to have been regions of high fertility.

one century after emancipation before the current rates of female single-headed households began to appear. It is the dramatic change combined with such a long lag after slavery that makes positing the usual links problematic. That the recent sharp increases in single-parent households occurred in a time of economic improvement is also puzzling. Works such as Herbert Gutman's (1976, discussed in Engerman 1978) point to the existence of a two-parent household under slavery, a point made earlier by the sociologist E. Franklin Frazier before he became influenced by observing the economic and family difficulties of the 1930s. There were other arguments about the impact of slavery on males and females such as those of W. E. Burghardt Du Bois (1909). Du Bois contended that the so-called "absent father" of the slave family need not have been physically absent, but he was forced to play a much weaker role in the family than did white fathers because of the controls imposed by masters. With the probable psychological costs to female slaves from forced sexual accessiblity by their masters, the two-parent slave household did not function in the same manner as did the free household. In the West Indies the single-parent household was more important in magnitude even at the time of emancipation, and its levels have long exceeded those in the United States, as has the share of illegitimate births (Roberts 1957, 263–306). In neither the United States nor the West Indies did the pattern of black family and gender relations both during and after slavery mirror the patterns in Africa prior to the transatlantic movement.[21] Thus freedom, leading to variations in constraints, did have significant effects, but not all its effects were evaluated positively by contemporaries and by subsequent scholars.[22]

Conclusion

This essay has used the systems of slavery and the transition from slavery to legal freedom of the previously enslaved to examine some of the issues raised about capabilities and freedom in Amartya Sen's *Development as Freedom*. The discussion of slavery reminds us that over the past two centuries human capabilities, as described by Sen, have increased in large measure because of the worldwide ending of slavery as a legal institution.

---

[21] The effect of planter policy on fertility is difficult to resolve. There were apparently more pro-natalist measures in the British West Indies than in the United States, possibly because they were thought more necessary there, given the lower fertility. Second, the decisions of women in one-parent vs. two-parent households may lead to differences in fertility, whether in slavery or in freedom.

[22] Thus it is debated whether the prevalence of the mother-headed household reflects a desired outcome or rather is the outcome of various forms of social problems.

individuals, but as discussed in the foregoing, so is survival for themselves and their children.

Voluntary slavery which existed in many times and places was used by different societies as a solution to perceived problems of overpopulation, and it was applied to adults as well as to children. In western Europe, however, where enslavement of other Europeans had been ended by the fourteenth century, excess births for the next centuries meant either abandonment, giving children to the church, or infanticide. Abandonment, at times, was based on socially accepted patterns that involved the expected retrieval of the children by members of the church or by individuals who would then provide the abandoned with permanent arrangements in exchange for labor. This was, in effect, a transfer of the rights to the child and its labor, at a zero selling price.

Voluntary slavery declined when incomes rose, as starvation became a more limited threat, and when more successful relief and welfare institutions by the state, the church, and by individuals were devised. It is clear, however, that under certain conditions the loss of freedom could be permanent, and was considered acceptable not only to the enslavers, but also to the enslaved.

The distinction between legal status and economic status, as well as between slave and free, was a central element in the debates on slavery in British colonies and in the United States in the early nineteenth century. It was claimed by proslavery advocates as well as by British workers (whatever their stance on abolishing slavery) that employers in Britain were able to force free workers to endure harsher working conditions, earn less income, and work longer hours than those of the West Indian slaves, backing these contentions with data from the two societies. And when it was argued that the British should encourage production of sugar by legally free laborers in India in the 1820s to replace the use of slave labor in the West Indies, the presumed benefits of free labor were questioned by pointing to the extremely low agricultural wages in India, and comparing free labor income in India with the consumption allowed slaves in the West Indies. It was not argued, of course, that all slaves had high standards of living or that many free workers might want to become slaves in order to benefit from improved living standards, but these cases do indicate that under certain rather important historical conditions slaves may have been better off materially than some free workers. This was so, even though the slaves obviously had the more limited legal freedom of choice.

II

While we generally regard slavery as a condition originating in compulsion and coercion, in many societies in Asia, Africa, and in pre-modern Europe, slavery was voluntarily entered into. Because of the low levels of

parents or relatives, from poverty and inability to maintain them in times of famine or of other general calamity, was the most prolific source of slavery and the origin of almost the whole slave population."

In China the traditional pattern was that "destitute parents, especially during bad harvest years," sold children, mostly females, since males were the source of parental support in their older ages (Watson 1980, 13). This was not an infrequent occurrence into the nineteenth and twentieth centuries, given the number of famines due to droughts and bad harvests that China experienced.

Similarly, in southeast Asia voluntary slavery was frequent, reflecting times of famine, shipwrecks, and conditions after the volcanic eruption of 1814 when "people would ask to be accepted as bondsmen in return for food." Indeed, according to Reid (1983, 159), "the ease with which these bonds were contracted was one of the things which most astonished foreign visitors to Southeast Asia."

In the Americas before Columbus, among the Aztecs (and the Mayans before them) there was self-sale, or sale of children or family members, "in time of hardship" to "secure survival." This is described by Clendinnen (1991, 99–100) as a circumstance in which "slavery provided a social net" "for those suffering gratuitous misfortunes," but also for those in this society who were regarded as "chronically shiftless individuals." She, however, rejects the contention that these were the slaves who were used for human sacrifice, claiming that activity was reserved for outsiders received as tribute or war captives.

Lovejoy's (1983, 70, 149) discussions of African slavery points to cases where, "in times of famine," children were sold and "self-enslavement to avoid starvation and the sale of children occurred to avoid the consequences of drought and famine." In their introductory essay to their edited volume *Slavery in Africa* Miers and Kopytoff (1977, 12) note "children and even sometimes adults were bartered for grain in times of famine to save the rest of the group." Cooper's (1977, 126) description of slavery on the east coast of Africa in the second half of the nineteenth century points to the large increase in the slave trade in 1884 due to "a devastating famine" which made people "desperate enough to sell their neighbors, their children, and even themselves in order to survive." Even later, in Africa, it was claimed that slaves themselves resisted "free" status when the latter resulted in lower standards of working and living, since some slaves did earn more than did the free population. Campbell and Alpers (2004) point to a case where slaves refused manumissions in order to maintain "their traditional privileges" and to avoid coercion doing "state imposed forced labor." Self-sale and sale of children at times of famine thus occurred in parts of Africa in the eighteenth, nineteenth, and twentieth centuries, if not earlier.

Pufendorf ([1688] 1934, 921, 936) argued that "In no case does it appear that nature allows a father to use his son as a pledge, or sell him, unless there is no other way to support him." In that case slavery should be "easy," and there should be some hope of becoming free. This would make enslavement provide a better outcome than if "he starve to death." Pufendorf also claimed "the beginnings of slavery followed upon the willing consent of men of poorer condition, and a contract in the form of 'goods for work,' " thus, "I will always provide for you, if you will always work for me."

Locke ([1690] 1963, 325–326), in contrast to Hobbes, argued that since man does not have power over his own life, he cannot "enslave himself to anyone" or "take away his life." Yet, he went on to argue, when enslaved if "he finds the hardship of his slavery outweigh the value of his life, 'tis in his power, by resisting the will of his master, to draw on himself the death he desires." Locke, in his drafting a constitution for the Carolinas, used the argument of a just war to justify Negro slavery. They had "forfeited their lives," and being without property, were outside of civil society.

Rousseau ([1762] 1947, 7, 8) argued against the possibility of a man enslaving himself, saying the "act is null and illegitimate," since whoever would attempt this was "out of his mind." The sale of children was also forbidden. He also redefined the issue of enslaving war captives, since there was, he argued, no "right to kill the conquered . . . deducible from the state of war." Yet Rousseau (9) did comment that a state at war with an enemy "has a right to kill its defenders, while they are bearing arms," but not once they surrender.

Blackstone, in his *Commentaries on the Laws of England* ([1765] 1979, 411, 412, 127), argued that slavery is "repugnant to reason, and the principles of natural law," and should not exist anywhere. Although the Justinian Code allowed the person's sale of himself, this could not be a valid contract, since there is no equivalent quid pro quo "for life, and liberty." He also argued against the customary argument justifying enslavement for war captives, since there was no longer a right to kill captives. Blackstone explained the absence of any acceptable form of voluntary slavery, since the English law "furnishes him with every thing necessary for their support." "All the necessities of life" would be provided by "means of the several statutes enacted for the relief of the poor," and based on "the more opulent part of the community." There was, in Blackstone, no belief in the Aristotelian natural slave, a slave due to his inferiority—physically, mentally, and morally.

Condorcet ([1781] 1999, 308, 313) regarded slavery as a crime "far worse than robbery." He denied the possibility of self-sale into slavery, that being an infringement of natural law. There were, however, conditions under which a person was "incapable of exercising his rights" and

Others included the belief that better physical and political treatment was possible as a slave, particularly for the elderly or mothers with children, as in the 1857 Georgia situation where it was believed that "a kind master was better able to provide and care for her than she was herself." The newspaper writer noted that the situation was "a nut for Yankee philosophers to crack" (Phillips 1909, 162; see also pp. 84–85, above).

Genovese (1974, 399, 401) comments that in the "late antebellum period and early war years, pressure mounted to induce free Negroes to reenslave themselves and to restrict their rights further." Few did, "but that some did suggests that often their legal and economic position was so precarious as to throw them on the mercy of a trusted white man." By 1860, nine southern states had legislation "allowing free persons of color to enslave themselves" (Morris 1996, 31–36).

Stampp (1956, 92–93, 216) argued that some Negroes might decline emancipation or seek a master since "given the general hostility toward free Negroes in both the North and South and the severe handicaps which they faced, the choice between 'freedom' and slavery did not always seem to be an altogether clear one." He states that the numbers reenslaving themselves by turning down emancipation was small, even though most southern states during the 1850s "adopted laws authorizing the voluntary enslavement of those people and enabling them to select their own masters."

V

The problem of voluntary slavery, and its long and frequent existence, does raise a number of important issues for the examination of slavery and emancipation. Were voluntary slaves treated better and made to suffer fewer psychological effects than were those forced into slavery? Patterson (1982, 27–28) states, "Voluntary servitude, however, was not slavery," but the case is made based on the need for protection within Ashanti society. In some cases of voluntary slavery children inherited the slave status, but not always. Should, on theoretical grounds, voluntary slaves be eligible to receive reparations, or should they reimburse their owners? Since voluntary slavery could lead to labor exploitation, should voluntary slaves then obtain the same benefits as involuntary slave labor? The nature of voluntary slaves poses the important question of the trade-offs between freedom and survival at low incomes, and the difficult choices imposed in societies where individuals received low incomes. The income levels of individuals will influence their behavior and helps define the meaning of freedom. Voluntary slavery has been one response to low incomes. Others include, government loans or expenditures, subsidized out-migration, and social redistribution schemes by individuals and

improvement in human welfare, and is to be encouraged. There are, however, several arguments against redeeming payments, both moral and practical. If slavery is regarded as robbery, being the theft of an individual, any payment is a reward to criminal activities, a reward to those performing the crime and not to its victims. Given, however, that slaves in most societies were regarded legally as property, and the current owners are not necessarily those involved in initial enslavement, recognition of property rights has generally been the policy followed at the time of emancipation. A more practical argument against redemption is that if done on a one at a time basis, this increase in the demand and the reduction in the supply of slaves will raise the price of slaves and make more enslavements profitable to sellers. Thus the number of slaves need not decline, new slaves replacing those freed. Central to the redemption scheme must then be a mechanism to prevent any new enslavement.

To place these points about redemption in context, it will be useful to look at the means by which past slavery has been ended. Individual freedoms have been the result of grants by owners, by self-purchase, or by purchases by third parties, whether antislavery organizations or, in the U.S. case, colonization societies. Manumissions were frequently accomplished by the right to self-purchase, not a grant of freedom by owners. Even in these societies in which manumission was more frequent than in the U.S. and British cases, it often entailed a payment by the slave out of his savings. Manumissions could be immediate or gradual, depending on the nature of the payment schemes. Runaways, if successful, were freed without redemption payments, a theft of self in response to the prior theft of enslavement. As seen in the case of Fredrick Douglass, runaways were liable to recapture if within the United States, and the only way to fully guarantee freedom was to redeem the slave from his owner.

In the Americas and elsewhere, most slave societies ended slavery, not by individual manumissions, but by legislation or, in the case of Haiti, by revolution. In most cases it was by the legislative ending of slavery, which came with some form of compensation paid to slaveowners, and no payment to slaves (see Engerman 1995). Similarly, the ending of European serfdom meant benefits to landowners and not to the serfs. The form of payment reflected the belief in these societies in the sanctity of property rights, as well as the nature of political power when legislation was passed. Compensation or redemption payments took several forms. It could be in the form of cash, bonds, or labor time. Under forms of gradual emancipation there was some compelled labor time that provided labor to the owners. A frequent form of gradual emancipation was to consider all born to slave mothers after a certain day as free, but required to remain with the mother's owner for 15 to 30 years, depending on the state or country. This was done to permit the owner to recover the costs of

Engerman, Stanley L. (1994), "Reflections on 'The Standard of Living' Debate: New Arguments and New Evidence," in John A. James and Mark Thomas (eds.), *Capitalism in Context: Essays on Economic Development and Cultural Change in Honor of R. M. Hartwell* (Chicago: University of Chicago Press), pp. 50–79.

Engerman, Stanley L. (1995), "Emancipations in Comparative Perspective: A Long and Wide View," in Gert Oostindie (ed.), *Fifty Years Later: Antislavery, Capitalism and Modernity in the Dutch Orbit* (Leiden: KITLV Press), pp. 223–241.

Engerman, Stanley L. (2000), "Comparative Approaches to the Ending of Slavery," in Howard Temperly (ed.), *After Slavery: Emancipation and its Discontents* (London: Frank Cass), pp. 281–300.

Fogel, Robert William (1989), *Without Consent or Contract: The Rise and Fall of American Slavery*. New York: W. W. Norton.

Fogel, Robert William, and Stanley L. Engerman (1974), *Time on the Cross: The Economics of American Negro Slavery*. Boston, MA: Little, Brown.

Franklin, John Hope, and Loren Schweninger (1999), *Runaway Slaves: Rebels on the Plantation*. New York: Oxford University Press.

Genovese, Eugene D. (1974), *Roll, Jordan, Roll: The World the Slaves Made*. New York: Pantheon.

Goldin, Claudia (1990), *Understanding the Gender Gap: An Economic History of American Women*. New York: Oxford University Press.

Grotius, Hugo ([1646] 1925), *The Law of War and Peace*. Oxford: Clarendon Press.

Gutman, Herbert G. (1976), *The Black Family in Slavery and Freedom, 1750–1925*. New York: Pantheon.

Hale, Robert (1952), *Freedom through Law: Public Control of Private Governing Power*. New York: Columbia University Press.

Hellie, Richard (1982), *Slavery in Russia, 1450–1725*. Chicago: University of Chicago Press.

Heuman, Gad, ed. (1985), "Out of the House of Bondage: Runaways, Resistance and Marronage in Africa and the New World." *Slavery and Abolition* 6(4).

Higman, B. W. (1984), *Slave Populations of the British Caribbean, 1807–1834*. Baltimore, MD: Johns Hopkins University Press.

Hobbes, Thomas ([1651] 1968), *Leviathan*. Baltimore: Penguin.

Holt, Sharon Ann (2000), *Making Freedom Pay: North Carolina Freedpeople Working for Themselves, 1865–1900*. Athens: University of Georgia Press.

Jones, Jacqueline (1985), *Labor of Love, Labor of Sorrow: Black Women, Work, and the Family from Slavery to the Present*. New York: Basic Books.

Locke, John ([1690] 1963), *Two Treatises of Government*. New York: Mentor Books.

Lovejoy, Paul E. (1983), *Transformations in Slavery: A History of Slavery in Africa*. Cambridge: Cambridge University Press.

Maine, Henry Sumner (1885), *Popular Government*. London: John Murray.

Mendelsohn, Isaac (1949), *Slavery in the Ancient Near East*. Oxford: Oxford University Press.

Miers, Suzanne, and Igor Kopytoff, eds. (1977), *Slavery in Africa: Historical and Anthropological Perspectives*. Madison: University of Wisconsin Press.

Steinfeld, Robert J. (2001), *Coercion, Contract, and Free Labor in the Nineteenth Century*. Cambridge: Cambridge University Press.

Temperley, Howard (1972), *British Antislavery, 1833–1870*. London: Longman.

Tolnay, Stewart E., and E. M. Beck (1995), *A Festival of Violence: An Analysis of Southern Lynchings, 1882–1930*. Urbana: University of Illinois Press.

Voltaire ([1768] 1994), *Political Writings*. Cambridge: Cambridge University Press.

Watson, James L. (1980), "Slavery as an Institution: Open and Closed Systems," in James L. Watson (ed.), *Asian and African Systems of Slavery* (Oxford: Basil Blackwell), pp. 1–15. See also pp. 233–250.

White, Deborah Gray (1985), *Ar'n't I a Woman? Female Slaves in the Plantation South*. New York: W. W. Norton.

on certain types of servile but seemingly voluntary labor arrangements. In many post-abolition situations (that is, where coerced labor is forbidden) freed slaves or serfs and other types of poor laborers were often recruited to enter into new types of tied labor contracts. These included indenture and other forms of bonded labor as well as labor-service tenancy arrangements that tied peasant access to land to an obligation to supply labor service to a landlord. While each of these voluntary contracts has the potential to enhance efficiency and may be *individually* rational to accept as has so often been stressed in the literature on "interlinked contracts" (Braverman and Stiglitz 1982; Bardhan 1989), we argue that once all general equilibrium interactions are considered, these contracts may paradoxically reduce welfare for laborers as a class. That is because tied contracts can act as a barrier to competition, limiting peasants' outside opportunities and therefore increasing the share of output that landlords can extract. In our model tied contracts or "servility" are "necessary" not because laborers are poor but rather as a strategy to help landlords sustain a collusive arrangement to pay workers wages below their marginal product and keep them poor. This can be seen by noting that an equally efficient (but less favorable to landlords) allocation of resources can be sustained via competitive factor markets without the need for any tying.

We employ a simple general equilibrium framework in which labor can be either free or coerced and where land and labor will be exchanged on markets that can be competitive or manipulated, perhaps via nonmarket collusive arrangements.[2] In addition to allowing us to analyze tied-labor contracts, the model will serve as a vehicle to formalize and reformulate some of the arguments and concerns that have animated the writings of Wakefield (1833), Marx (1887), Nieboer (1910), Domar (1970), and others regarding the relationships between conditions of labor scarcity and the "need" or demand for institutions of coerced labor. By working with variants of the same basic model under different assumptions about initial economy-wide factor endowments and asset ownership, we can compare equilibrium distributional outcomes under different institutional and contractual arrangements, including markets with free labor and free tenancy, slavery, and tenancy arrangements with labor-service obligations. This last type of arrangement has been ubiquitous throughout history (Morner 1970) and it was quite central to the organization of production under serfdom. Even today labor tying is seen in many regions of the developing world, and a careful analysis of this case offers important clues for understanding the origin and nature of other servile, yet seemingly voluntary, labor arrangements including several forms of bonded labor.

---

[2] The presentation builds upon and extends Conning (2005).

circumstances a ban on child or bonded labor may then lead the equilibrium adult wage to rise by enough that households no longer choose child or bonded labor. In these models the role of policy is to help the economy coordinate around a new Pareto-superior equilibrium. In our model the role of bans or regulations is to challenge the power of local elites by disrupting their strategies to restrict the choices of the poor and prevent peasant income from rising closer to its competitive level. Policy may improve the freedoms and the welfare of the poor, but there is less obvious scope for Pareto improvements compared to these other models, and output may well fall rather than rise. In short where these others are models of coordination failure, ours is fundamentally a model of conflict over property rights and freedoms.

Before examining the details of the model framework, the next section places our analysis within a broader academic literature on unfree labor. This section reviews some of the arguments that have been made for why the *material* well-being of unfree laborers might fall following emancipation and why a ban on bonded labor and other forms of voluntary servitude could also do more harm than good. We turn then to the presentation of a simple general equilibrium model designed to pinpoint how different institutions of unfree labor might emerge as factor endowments, technology, and distribution of resources in an economy change.

Debates over Unfree Labor

Free and unfree persons are quite different. Even in very poor societies, free persons are typically able to choose their place of residence, seek work with more than one employer, accumulate property, and seek credit and insurance from the most favorable source. They can also make choices about whether to sleep late, chat the morning away, enjoy or refuse the company of others if they so desire, and consume unhealthy beverages during breaks from work. Unfree laborers rarely enjoy these freedoms except in stolen moments or at the whim and discretion of their masters or employers.

Unfree persons are those persons constrained by forced labor arrangements such as slavery or serfdom, or by "voluntary" but servile labor relationships such as indentured or debt-bonded labor. Persons in these various categories have lost part of the everyday control over time and body that is so characteristic of the free person. Often with the explicit sanction of laws and societal norms, these individuals have found their opportunities for advancement sharply limited by the obligation to remain at the constant beck and call of their masters or employers. Even today, according to a 2005 ILO report, as many as 12.3 million people worldwide remain trapped in unfree labor relationships.

The second component of the argument for caution examines present and past economies, suggesting they may not involve coercion. In this view historical and present-day arrangements such as serfdom, share-cropping, labor-service tenancy, and other "tied" labor arrangements are not self-evidently the result of the application of force by the employer, as many have claimed. Rather, these may perhaps be contractual adaptations that help individuals sustain commitments in a milieu where asymmetric information, costly enforcement, and the absence of effective and impartial courts make commitments difficult or costly to sustain.

Hundreds of thousands of poor European migrants, for example, used indentured servitude contacts to finance their passage to the Americas in the seventeenth and eighteenth centuries (Bush 2000; Galenson 1984). Often after five years of service the indentured servant earned his "freedom dues" and became a settler and possible property owner. These poor Europeans did not possess sufficient resources to finance the voyage and purchase land and did not have assets to pledge to assure a lender of compensation in the event of default. Given the distances and arduous passage, and the ease of movement to an ever-expanding frontier, lenders had reason to fear that loans would not be repaid. In this environment, voluntary relinquishment of rights for a temporary period of time seemed quite reasonable; a lender could sell the loan to an employer in the New World who might then collect repayment out of wages. The penal code helped enforce these contracts. A ban on indentured servitude would have made worse off the poor European workers who could not afford the voyage. By similar argument, a harsh penal code could be defended in the name of helping the poor to hold to commitments that would help improve their lot.

Studies by Bauer (1979) and Knight (1986) of debt bonding in Latin American agriculture and larger comparative surveys by Northrup (1995) and Bush (2000) each emphasize the ways in which these contracts often responded to migrants' and peasant farmers' economic demands and often led to their advancement, even if they do agree that abuses did often occur. In a similar vein, North and Thomas (1973) saw serfdom emerging as a contractual arrangement that exchanged "labor services in return for the lord's protection" and other public goods in a dangerous world (p. 20). They rationalized the labor-service component of these contracts as a substitution for money rents in an incompletely monetized economy.

While many discussions on indentured servitude and serfdom have been broadly empirical in approach, a related debate on labor tenancy has been largely theoretical. The issue has been to show why tenants had to deliver labor services as payment for a plot of land in replacement for, or in addition to, monetary rent. The basic argument is that, in a world of

landowners withhold land from the lease market, giving rise to a "lati-fundia-minifundia" agrarian structure.

This framework will permit a quick tour of several hypotheses and debates that have engaged political economists, economists, and historians for a long time. For example, we will state and analyze the Nieboer-Domar hypothesis on the causes of slavery or serfdom and mention some elements of its critiques. The model also provides a framework for understanding debates concerning the economic and political consequences of emancipation and the nature of the transitions or "paths" toward more free and competitive land and labor contracts (Byres 1996; de Janvry 1981).

We begin with an economy that has $\bar{T} = 100$ units of land. There are $M = 2$ identical landlord households that together own 80 percent ($\theta = 0.8$) of the total land area, or 40 units of land each. There are also $N = 80$ peasant households that together own (or have customary property rights to) the remaining 20 percent of the land mass, or 0.25 units per household. Each peasant household owns $H = 1.25$ units of household labor, and for simplicity we assume landlords do not supply manual labor. The total labor force consists therefore of $\bar{L} = N \cdot H = 100$ units of labor, and the over all land-to-labor ratio is $\bar{t} = \bar{T}/\bar{L} = 1$ unit of land per laborer.

Landlord and peasant households have knowledge of the same crop production technology that would allow them to produce a staple agricultural product sold at unit price set by world markets. In our first scenario, we assume that landlords begin with a higher initial endowment of nontraded farm management skills. Farm production technology is summarized by a standard constant-returns-to-scale (CRS) Cobb-Douglas production function $q = T^{\alpha}L^{\beta}S^{1-\alpha-\beta}$, where T and L are land and labor farm inputs and S is the household's holding of a *nontraded* farming skill or labor supervision ability. By normalizing the peasant's endowment of factor S to $S_p = 1$, we can represent the peasant's technology more compactly by the restricted production function $F(T,L) = T^{\alpha}L^{\beta}$, which, as long as S plays any significant role in production (i.e., as long as $\alpha + \beta < 0$), will display decreasing returns to scale in land and labor input. The importance of nontraded skills in agricultural production is empirically well grounded and is widely used to explain the lasting prevalence of family farming and tenancy in many contexts (Hayami and Otsuka 1993).

Landlords employ the same production technology but have a larger endowment of the nontraded input, $S_r > 1$. The landlord's technology can then be represented as $G(T,L) = A \cdot F(T,L)$ where $A = S_r^{(1-\alpha-\beta)}$. Intuitively, the landlord's assumed higher level of managerial skill can be thought of as raising the productivity of the land and labor inputs in the

by the *overall* land-to-labor ratio and the distribution of *nontraded* factors. Factor prices, equal to marginal products, are easily calculated to be

$$w = F_L(\bar{t}, 1) = \beta \left[\, \bar{t}\, \right]^{\alpha}$$
$$r = F_T(\bar{t}, 1) = \alpha \left[\, \bar{t}\, \right]^{\alpha - 1}$$
$$\pi = (1 - \alpha - \beta)\left[\, \bar{t}\, \right]^{\alpha}$$

where w, r, and π are, respectively the market wage and rental rates and the shadow price of a unit of nontraded S. This last quantity is also the value of peasant farm profits. The wage rate w increases monotonically with $\bar{t}$ as labor becomes scarcer (or, what is the same thing, as land becomes more abundant) while the competitive land market rental rate falls. Total income to household g is given by the sum of farm profits plus factor sales:

$$\Pi_g(\bar{t}, 1) = S_g \left[F(\bar{t}, 1) - r\bar{t} - w1 \right] + w\overline{L}_g + r\overline{T}_g$$

At an initial land-to-labor ratio of $\bar{t} = 1$, landlords in our simulated economy will be essentially rentiers, deriving 95 percent of their income, or 19 units, from their 40 units of land valued at the market rental rate $r = 0.45$, and only 5 percent, or one unit of income, from farm profits.

Since all farms face a common market wage, a peasant laborer should be, on the margin, indifferent between working another hour for a landlord or on her own farm or tenancy. This implies that there should be no compelling reason for any party to tie labor and tenancy contracts. Some peasants might of course rent from and work for the same landlord, but this would emerge by chance. Landlords might want to clock their laborers' hours on the job (one could perhaps interpret S as a required input into this monitoring process), but a landlord should not care at all about what any given laborer does on her own family farm or tenancy on her own time. This is because each hour of work that that laborer withdraws from the landlord can be easily and immediately replaced by hiring another laborer at the same spot market wage.

Labor Scarcity and Coerced Labor: The Nieboer-Domar Hypothesis

Suppose that, due to discovery or conquest, the economy's land endowment is now expanded from 100 to $\bar{t} > 100$ units, while the labor force remains constant at ($\overline{L} = 100$). Assume furthermore that it is either the

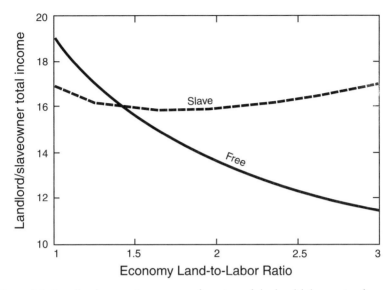

Figure 5.1 Landlord sector income as a function of the land-labor ratio: free markets vs. slavery.

plantations in the Americas and the US South" (p. 19). We do agree with the criticism that Domar, much like Wakefield (1833) and Nieboer (1910) before him, appears at times to suggest that landlords' incentive to clamp down on laborer's mobility is largely due to the existence of an open frontier to which peasants might otherwise be drawn to set up independent farms. In fact, an open frontier is not an essential element of the argument. As suggested by the model above, what will matter more generally is the distribution of property rights over land as well as anything else that might affect the value of laborers' outside opportunities.[4]

Domar was not very clear about the nature of the difference between slavery and serfdom or about how technology or the initial distribution of property rights over land might shape these institutional choices and transformations. To clarify these issues, consider the following simple extension which models the imposition of slavery in a very crude way.

Suppose that landlords can, as a result of a campaign of violence and intimidation, kidnap *half* the existing peasant population and compel them to supply their labor at a subsistence wage $\underline{w}$ per unit. We assume

[4] The argument that an open frontier is not essential was also made by Engerman (1973) and was an essential element of Marx's elaborate critique of Wakefield in the last chapter of *Capital*, volume I.

Figure 5.1 compares landlord income under an economy with free tenancy and free labor market arrangements as earlier analyzed (solid line) to that under a slave economy where slave laborers can be compelled to work but do not use nontraded skills S (dashed line) for different land-to-labor ratios.[5] As computed with the parameters given above, landlords earn higher incomes in the free economy when the land-to-labor ratio is somewhere approximately below 1.25, but prefer the slave economy in more labor-scarce environments. This comparison does not net out the costs that slaveowners might have to pay to coerce a slave labor force, nor does it consider the possibility that slave laborers could be either more or less productive than free laborers.[6] As drawn, landlord incomes at first fall but later rise as the land-labor ratio increases. This reflects the tug of war between falling income from land rents and rising income from owning slaves.

The dispossession and enslavement of half of the peasant population means that land and labor that these households had employed in a free economy are now put on the market for the remaining production units to absorb. In the new "efficient" equilibrium, the size of landlord farms and the remaining free farms must expand proportionately to absorb these resources, both wages and land rental rates must fall (factor productivity falls as less S is being used), and farm profits must rise (as S is now more scarce). Total output would fall compared to an efficient free and competitive equilibrium.[7] Independent farm producers who are not enslaved may either gain or lose from this change in factor prices, depending on the importance of wages and farm profits in total household income. The political implications of this analysis are rather interesting. It suggests for example a reason why white small-farm producers in the

---

[5] The parameters are as described so far in the text and $\underline{w} = 0.45$, the free labor market wage when $\bar{t} = 1$. Raising w simply raises the costs of owning each slave, lowering landlord income in the slave economy and therefore raising the cutoff level of $\bar{t}$ above which slavery becomes financially more lucrative.

[6] A large and important literature has debated this latter question. Adam Smith and many abolitionists often argued that slave labor was by its very nature less efficient than free labor because a slave who could not own and accumulate property would have less incentive to supply quality labor. Several nineteenth-century political economists challenged this view (Drescher 2002). Fitting into this debate, Fogel and Engerman (1974) have argued that slave labor in the antebellum South produced more output per worker than free labor because of the extra labor and "economies of scale" that they argue could be achieved under a coercive gang labor system. The dominant view amongst economic historians seems to be that American slavery was on the whole a profitable institution to slaveowners at the time of its abolition (Kolchin 2003). Our model can be easily adapted to either assumption.

[7] If slaveowners could extract sufficiently more output per worker from a slave than from a free person through coercion, then total measured output could fall following the abolition of slavery, the explanation suggested by Fogel and Engerman (1974). Without denying that this effect could have been important, we shall suggest a complementary explanation.

of equilibrium. Suppose slavery or serfdom were suddenly abolished. To add a touch of realism, suppose also that the transition were somewhat disruptive so that for a brief period households retreated to a semiautarkic equilibrium. Recall that the "slave economy" of the last section was privately profitable to the slaveowners but it was also inefficient in so far as slaves' nontraded skills S were not being utilized. Whether this efficiency cost is large or small depends on the importance of S in production and the extent to which S is held by slaves.

Rather than allow the emergence of a competitive market where landlords have to compete for labor by offering the highest wage or for tenants by offering the lowest land rent, they would much prefer a more collusive arrangement. Consider the following collusive contracting arrangement: landlords agree to divide up the peasant population equally amongst themselves and to not contract with each other's peasants. Each landlord then offers each peasant household a take-it-or-leave-it contract with the following clauses:

The landlord will lease $T_p^e = \bar{t}$ units of land (i.e., the efficient level described in the competitive equilibrium above) to a peasant in exchange for a lump-sum rent or tribute payment R (value set as described below).

The lease is provided on condition that the tenant additionally agrees to supply 0.25 units of *labor service* to the landlord.

The tenant shall not sublease or allow any other workers to work the land without the landlord's explicit consent.

To insure that the contract remains an entirely voluntary transaction for the peasant, the landlord cannot set the tribute payment R above a level that would push the tenant-laborer's welfare below their reservation utility, or what they could earn elsewhere if they refused the contract. The peasant's reservation utility depends on the availability of alternate contracting opportunities and his ownership of land (defined broadly to include customary land rights or access to common property areas). If all other peasants in the economy are accepting similar contracts, then the only alternative to contracting with the landlord becomes to remain or retreat into autarkic (Chayanovian) production. In either case, the most a peasant household can earn is what it could get from using its available land and labor endowments. In our numeric example this would mean devoting $\bar{T}_p = 0.125$ and $L_p = 1.25$, to home production to yield income $F(\bar{T}_p, \bar{L}_p)$.[8] To assure voluntary participation the tribute rent R must be chosen to make sure that the peasant earns slightly more from accepting than from rejecting the contract:

$$F(\bar{t},1) - R \geq F(\bar{T}_p, \bar{L}_p)$$

of labor time or effort could not be perfectly observed on the landlord's farm, the situation would essentially become a classic principal-agent or moral hazard problem. The landlord would complain that his peasants lacked a work ethic and were diverting resources to their individual plots rather than fulfilling their contractually agreed-upon legal obligations to provide labor service. Landlords as employers would also argue, again on seemingly firm liberal grounds, about the need to maintain a system of criminal sanctions against contract breach (Steinfeld 2001). How, after all, could free markets be made to function properly unless workers could be kept to their promises, and how could this be for anything but for the workers own good, when they entered into these contracts of their own free will?

Without legal enforcement, the argument would go, landlords might have little choice but to respond to this situation of moral hazard by underinvesting in agriculture and rationing peasants to smaller-than-efficient tenancies, with a consequent fall in total output. This moral hazard problem is a very familiar one that has been at the center of important explanations of the choice of contract forms. The crucial point to note here however is that the "problem" emerges primarily as a consequence of the fact that landlords are trying to get away with paying labor a wage far below its marginal product. Since the wage for each extra hour of work on the landlords' *demesne* is essentially zero, peasants are strongly tempted to cut back on an hour of labor service and divert that labor to their own tenancy, where on the margin they earn $F_T(\bar{t}, 1)$. A peasant therefore has strong incentives to feign sickness or find other ways to cut back on labor-service hours.[9] There is no similarly strong incentive to avoid wage labor in a competitive economy, because the marginal gain peasants earn by using that labor on their own farm would then be exactly offset by the wage $w = F_T(\bar{t}, 1)$ they lose by working an hour less for the landlord.

Can this collusive equilibrium be sustained? The terms of the contract act as a barrier to competition for several reasons. Clearly stipulated and strictly enforced labor-service obligations aim at stopping labor from being diverted to peasant plots as well as to other landlords. In actual practice a way to control labor's outside opportunities was to mark class differences and insist that the servant adopt a servile and deferential attitude and to remain attentive to the master's every "beck and call." Although historians have sometimes sought to root such behaviors in cultural and military traditions, these behaviors obviously also served the

---

[9] The landlord cannot ameliorate the problem by offering a larger tenancy (and hence residual claimancy) to the laborer and then extract rents through a higher lump-sum tribute payment, because this would fail to fully utilize the landlord's own farming skill S.

note in which they agreed to pay off their obligation by serving the land-lord as a servant or a labor-service tenant (Kliuchevsky 1968). It was not unusual for a contract to have a worker "serve for usury," or in other words, work merely to pay off the accumulation of interest, leaving the level of the principal or the bond unchanged. Any pledger who broke service or was declared insolvent by a court could be turned into a per-manent bondsman who could then only be freed at his master's will, a condition of service that became hereditary. These arrangements still re-mained "voluntary" and contractual so long as the law generally allowed the peasant to ransom his or her freedom and, although only during offi-cially sanctioned days of the year, to change employers.

This system of voluntary bonding evolved into bondage in perpetuity or involuntary serfdom over the course of the late sixteenth and seven-teenth centuries as new laws were introduced that made it increasingly difficult for peasants to change employers or to ransom their freedom. V. O. Kliuchevsky saw these restrictions as a landlord reaction to the conditions of "acute labor shortage" that developed as "masses of the peasantry" started to flee the central Russian provinces in search of land and opportunities in the newly expanded frontier" (Kliuchevsky 1968, 182).[11]

As this discussion suggests, the dividing line between voluntary and in-voluntary tied labor contracts has oftentimes been blurred. Economists often assume that a system of voluntary contracts must, almost by defini-tion, lead to improvements to the laborers who accept them, yet as we have argued here this need not be the case once the possibility of landlord collusion and general equilibrium interactions are considered.

History is replete with other examples of laws and state action aimed at facilitating collusion amongst landlords to keep "voluntary" labor arrangements from becoming too competitive (Binswanger, Deininger, and Feder 1995). For example, after the Thirteenth Amendment to the Constitution was adopted in 1865 banning involuntary servitude in the United States, southern legislatures rushed to immediately pass "Black Codes" to limit freed slaves' outside opportunities by making it more dif-ficult for them to switch employers, own land, access forests and other common property resources, or even to remain idle. This legislation was often quite naked in its obvious attempts to sustain collusive arrangements.

---

[11] Kliuchevsky underscores how landlords used the legal device of debt bonding to tie down their workers, for instance by converting practically all the remaining servants who had previously worked for wages and without promissory notes into bondsmen. The terms of bondsmen's contracts also became more and more onerous as time passed, adding clauses in which bondsmen had to for example agree to "live as a peasant under my master for the rest of my life and not run away anywhere," and which obliged the peasant to now pay damages on top of his debt for leaving (Kliuchevsky 1968, 184).

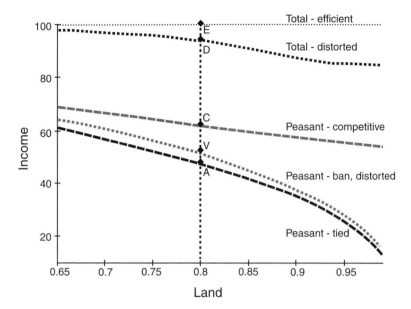

Figure 5.2 Total income and peasant sector income under different regimes.

given by the sum of farm profits plus the market value of factors owned—is as indicated by the solid line labeled "Peasant—competitive" passing through point C. This has a slope of minus the competitive rental rate on land r because the value of land owned by peasants declines as the fraction of total land owned by landlords θ increases. Point C on the diagram indicates that when landlords own 80 percent of the land stock, the peasant sector nonetheless still takes home 62 percent of total income in the economy by virtue of their ownership of labor and other factors.[13]

Under a collusive arrangement of tied contracts, peasant incomes could in principle be pressed down to their autarky levels. That would leave the peasant sector earning just slightly more than they would from withdrawing from transactions with landlords and instead making use of their own land $(\bar{T}_p = (1 - \theta)\bar{T}/N)$ and labor (H) resources. This would earn them their Chayanovian farm income $F(\bar{T}_p, H)$. Point A indicates that at $\theta = 0.8$, where the typical peasant household has access to $\bar{T}_p = 0.25$ units of land, this income would be $F(0.25, 1.25) = 47.4$, which is considerably below their income with competitive markets.

---

[13] Recall that the efficient competitive equilibrium had $w = r = 0.45$. Total imputed income from the peasant sectors' ownership of 20 units of land is therefore $9 = 0.45 \times 20$, their income from owning 100 units of labor is $45 = .45 \times 100$, and total farm profits (or returns to the nontraded S) from the 80 peasant farms equals $8 = 0.1 \times 80$. This sums to 62.

a distorted one with lower total output and only a scant improvement in peasant welfare. The argument, which is laid out in some more detail in the appendix and in Conning (2005), is that landlords' reaction to a ban that deprives them of the use of tied contracts as an efficient mechanism for surplus extraction may be to turn to other privately profitable but socially inefficient mechanisms to earn rents.

As discussed above, elites frequently acted to close down the outside income–generating opportunities of their newly untied laborers using both legal and illegal means. Our argument here is that that landlords would likely also seek to limit peasants' outside opportunities via economic *market* mechanisms, without the need for (but in practice very likely in addition to) this kind of extra-economic barrier building.[15]

Suppose that following emancipation the economy temporarily moved to the competitive equilibrium indicated by C in figure 5.2. Starting from this efficient outcome, can landlords change resource allocations to raise their incomes? If landlords control a large enough amount of land, the answer is they can. Consider the simplest case where our $M = 2$ landlords collude but cannot use tied contracts, so they must transact at "market" wages and rental rates.[16] As discussed previously, competitive landlords would be rentiers, as the bulk of their income is from leasing out large amounts of land to tenants, and only secondarily from farm profits. If in such a context landlords have enough land to be able to exploit market power, they should limit the amount of land they lease to the market to push up land rents. This is the classic partial-equilibrium argumentation for a monopoly markup on land rents. But in this general equilibrium context there is an additional important effect that landlords must also consider. Landlords maximize profits plus the value of owned land. As they restrict land leased out, they increase earnings from land but also end up pushing down available land per worker in the peasant sector. With less land to work with, the marginal product of labor declines on peasant farms, leading peasant households to optimally increase their supply of labor to the market at any given wage. Since landlords are the largest (and in our constructed case, the only) net employer of wage labor, this benefits them by increasing profits. In short, the exercise of monopoly power over land also creates monopsony rents from labor.

---

[15] In this sense the model offers microfoundations to help explain the pattern of elite behavior described by Ransom and Sutch and others, by providing a framework within which to identify and quantify the costs and rewards elites stood to gain via political and economic actions. It also offers a microeconomic explanation for the kind of inverse relationship between asset inequality and political and economic outcomes that Sokoloff and Engerman (2000) and others have identified in explaining the divergent growth paths of regions.

[16] Similar results, albeit in somewhat more muted form, emerge if we instead model landlord interaction as a noncooperative Cournot game (Conning 2005).

Engerman's (1974) for the U.S. South that coerced labor produced more output per hour than free labor. Our model shows that the size of the output collapse and the resulting level of peasant welfare following emancipation, are affected by several factors including the initial distribution of property rights over land, the ability of elites to collude and of peasants to organize, and the role of the nontraded factor S.

Consider further the role of land inequality. While the efficient way to produce 100 units in our numerical example was to allocate 80 percent of total production to peasant farms and the remaining 20 percent to landlords, simple simulations for our benchmark parameters show landlord farms expanding to account for more than 50 percent of output at $\theta = 0.8$ and expanding ever more rapidly at higher levels. As one increases θ to higher and higher levels, tenancy suppression becomes more active until the point where (at around $\theta = 0.87$) landlords find it optimal to close down the tenancy market completely. At this point, landlords decide that they earn more from monopsony rents on labor (since they have pushed the market wage far below the marginal product of a hired laborer), and they simply ignore land rent earnings (Conning 2005).

At yet higher levels of initial land concentration η, simulations show that landlords will actually start to encroach on peasant lands via reverse tenancy—large landlords will be observed hiring in land from small landholders. This behavior may make sense in a model where we have assumed that peasant property rights to land are scrupulously protected by the state, since landlords then only have markets to use as a strategy to manipulate factor prices and obtain the land they desire. In more realistic contexts, where property rights cannot be assumed to be costlessly enforced by a third party, one is likely to instead see the flaring up of conflict, for example land-hungry peasants squatting on landlord farms and common lands, or perhaps landlords hiring thugs not only to drive off squatters but also to restrict peasant access to frontier lands.[17] One might interpret the drive to enclose common lands as responding in part to a similar logic.

The discussion suggests that an "American road" trajectory, with active tenancy markets and prosperous family farmers, is likely to take root only following emancipation or the opening of a new frontier where land is distributed in a more egalitarian fashion (θ is low). A more distorted "Prussian road" such as that followed in Russia, Prussia, and many parts of Latin America, where landlords suppress tenancy and land sale markets, is more likely when initial land inequality is high.

[17] Conning and Robinson (2007) explore a related model that shows how endogenously determined property rights conflicts would further suppress the operation of market for tenancies.

at times good reasons to regulate the freedom of contract. Prohibiting a landlord and a peasant from contracting would appear to stand in the way of obvious gains from trade. Yet in a purely competitive market there is no need for tied contracts, and use of tying by landlords may point to an attempt to control laborers' outside opportunities. A prohibition on tying may result in less efficient collusive arrangements but can deliver a greater share of the lower output to the hands of the laborers.

This is another example of the general theory of the second-best that is well used in economics: where labor markets may not be competitive to begin with and where other markets (e.g., for insurance) may not be perfect, government regulation or banning of certain voluntary contracts may improve general well-being or redistribute well-being in socially desirable ways. Stopping one household from using bonding or child labor worsens their welfare, but a uniform ban on bonded labor contracts (Genicot 2002) or child labor can produce general equilibrium effects that may lead to a better equilibrium (Basu 1999; Baland and Robinson 2000). Our explanation is related to existing arguments, yet in an important sense is also fundamentally different. Each of these other accounts focuses on externalities on labor and/or credit markets and the role of public policy in helping to solve the coordination failures that may prevent society from reaching a Pareto-superior equilibrium where every member of society can in principle be made better off. Our account focuses on the *strategic* action of local power holders to actively limit the outside opportunities of laborers.[18] Society must overcome not a coordination problem but rather the local power structures that restrict the choices of the poor and prevent peasant welfare from rising closer to its competitive level.

The discussion of an exception to the intuition that free contracts are invariably socially desirable should not make one sanguine about public policy. Governments are more likely to be handmaids of welfare-worsening institutions regulating labor relations, as in Russia, where the state prevented serfs from changing employers.

The analysis of freedom and contracting in the context of labor must proceed dialectically, asking how an initial distribution of freedom and property generates a pattern of contracts, and how this pattern might then change subsequently. A famine might induce many laborers to willingly become serfs; their serf status may drive down the wage in the normal, nonfamine economy, inducing still more laborers to enter serfdom. An expanding frontier might induce laborers to leave their ancestral homes and employers in search of higher returns. Their former

---

[18] Basu (1986) explores similar ideas in his analysis of examples of "triadic" power. Our approach allows for potentially more general comparative predictions across economies by virtue of being embedded within a more canonical neoclassical general equilibrium framework.

$L_r^s = 10L_p^s$, and land market equilibrium now requires

$$2 \cdot 10T_p^s + 40T_p^s = \overline{T}$$

$$T_p^s = \frac{\overline{T}}{60} = \frac{10}{6}\overline{t}$$

A similar calculation using the labor market equilibrium equation reveals that $L_p^s = 10/6 = 1.67$. The institution of slavery blocks 40 households from becoming direct producers, which then makes room for each of the remaining farm units to expand approximately 67 percent compared to the equilibrium without slavery. Wage rates and rentals must fall as slaves' nontraded farming skills are no longer being utilized as in the competitive economy.

The Market-power Distorted Economy When Landlords Cannot Tie

When tying is not allowed landlords must hire-in labor at a "market" wage w and land rental rate r. A "landlord cartel" would however collude to distort resource allocations to manipulate prices to their advantage. They would act to choose factor use on the typical landlord farm (T_r, L_r) to maximize

$$\left[G(T_r, L_r) - r(T_r, L_r) \cdot T_r - w(T_r, L_r) \cdot L_r \right] + r(T_r, L_r)\theta\overline{T} / M$$

Market labor wage w and the land rental rate r will be determined by the marginal product of labor $w = F_L(T_p, L_p)$ and the marginal product of land $r = F_T(T_p, L_p)$ on the competitive fringe of peasant farms. In the expression above we have written w and r as a function of T_r and L_r, by using the factor market balance equations, $T_p = \overline{T}/N - MT_r/N$ and $L_p = \overline{L}/N - ML_r/N$. Market factor prices are determined by the marginal productivity of factors on peasant farms, but these will be manipulated prices because landlords will take into account how their own production choices affect the price and availability of land and labor in the peasant sector. The pair of equations that make up the first-order conditions for this problem are highly nonlinear, but the optimal solutions to maximize landlord cartel income are easily found numerically for given parameter values, as discussed in the text.

Bibliography

Akerlof, George A. (1976), "The Economics of Caste and of the Rat Race and Other Woeful Tales," *Quarterly Journal of Economics* 90(4): 599–617.

Edmonds, Eric, and Pavcnik, Nina (2005), "Child Labor in the Global Economy," *Journal of Economic Perspectives* 18(1): 199–220.

Engerman, Stanley (1973), "Some Considerations Relating to Property Rights in Man," *Journal of Economic History* 33: 43–65.

Fogel, Robert William, and Stanley Engerman (1974), *Time on the Cross: The Economics of American Negro Slavery*. Boston: Little Brown.

Galenson, David W. (1984), *White Servitude in Colonial America: An Economic Analysis*. New York: Cambridge University Press.

Genicot, Garance (2002), "Bonded Labor and Serfdom: A Paradox of Voluntary Choice," *Journal of Development Economics* 67(1): 101–127.

Goldin, Claudia (1988), "Maximum Hours Legislation and Female Employment: A Reassessment," *Journal of Political Economy* 96: 189–205.

Goldin, Claudia (1991), "Marriage Bars: Discrimination against Married Women Workers, 1920 to 1950," in H. Rosovsky, D. Landes, and P. Higgonet (eds.), *Favorites of Fortune: Technology, Growth, and Economic Development since the Industrial Revolution* (Cambridge, MA: Harvard University Press), pp. 511–536.

Hart, G. (1986), "'Interlocking Transactions: Obstacles, Precursors or Instruments of Agrarian Capitalism?" *Journal of Development Economics* 23 (1): 173–203.

Hayami, Yujiro, and Keijiro Otsuka (1993), *The Economics of Contract Choice: An Agrarian Perspective*. Oxford: Oxford University Press.

Holmstrom, Bengt, and Paul Milgrom (1990), "Regulating Trade among Agents," *Journal of Institutional and Theoretical Economics* 146(1): 85–105.

ILO (2005), "A Global Alliance against Forced Labour: Global Report under the Follow-up to the ILO Declaration on Fundamental Principles and Rights at Work," in *93rd Session 2005, Report I (B)*: International Labour Office.

Kandori, Michihiro (1992), "Social Norms and Community Enforcement," *Review of Economic Studies* 59: 61–80.

Kliuchevsky, V. O. (1968), *A Course in Russian History: The Seventeenth Century*. Chicago: Quadrangle Books.

Knight, Alan (1986), "Mexican Peonage: What Was It and Why Was It?" *Journal of Latin American Studies* 18: 41–74.

Kolchin, Peter (1987), *Unfree Labor: American Slavery and Russian Serfdom*. Cambridge: Harvard University Press.

Kolchin, Peter (2003), *American Slavery, 1619–1877*. New York: Hill and Wang.

Krugman, Paul (1997), "In Praise of Cheap Labor: Bad Jobs at Bad Wages Are Better than No Jobs at All," *Slate*, 20 March 1997.

Lundahl, Mats (1992), *Apartheid in Theory and Practice: An Economic Analysis*. Boulder, CO: Westview Press.

Marx, Karl (1887), *Capital*, vol. I: *The Process of Production of Capital*. Moscow: Progress Publishers.

Morner, Magnus (1970), "A Comparative Study of Tenant Labor in Parts of Europe, Africa and Latin America 1700–1900: A Premiliary Report of a Research Project in Social History," *Latin American Research Review* 5(2): 3–15.

Nieboer, Herman Jeremias (1910), *Slavery as an Industrial System: Ethnological Researches*. The Hague: M. Nijhoff.

Part II

ANTHROPOLOGICAL CONSIDERATIONS

Chapter Six

Slavery and Slave Redemption in Sudan

JOK MADUT JOK

As I read the thoughtful pieces by my co-contributors in this volume, I am struck by the complexity of attempting to apply the terms of debate about the "effects" of slave redemption to the particularities of the Sudanese experience. That this is so, applies as to the nonacademic protagonists in the debate as much as to anyone else.

Throughout the late 1990s, when the reemergence of slavery and slave redemption in Sudan were hotly debated issues, especially in the United States as well as in Sudan, one of the main characters in this drama was the government of Sudan, which argued bitterly against the claims that slavery is practiced in Sudan. Upon the realization that these abduction and enslavement issues were too embarrassing internationally, the government of Sudan felt that it needed a body to respond to the allegations in a more concerted way. It set up an organization known as the Committee for the Eradication of Abduction of Women and Children (CEAWAC). Despite the documented involvement of the government itself in raiding, abduction, and enslavement, CEAWAC came to the defense of the government and tried to explain away the whole phenomenon as the work of detractors who wanted to smear the good name of the Islamic government in Khartoum. The "Americans" and the "Zionists" were named in the mission to defame Sudan.

Another character in the debate was Christian Solidarity International (CSI), a Zurich-based evangelical organization that underwrote most of the slave redemption programs and whose representative actually traveled to south Sudan on a rather frequent basis to undertake the actual buying back of the slaves through Arab intermediaries to secure their freedom. Conducted clandestinely and without clear methods of verification by independent researchers or journalists, CSI's work became the subject of concern for those who regard slave redemption as a well-intentioned practice but one which can invigorate slavery, as it promotes slave-taking by providing the market for abductees.

Other influential parties contributing to this debate were two child welfare agencies, United Nations Children's Fund (UNICEF) and Save the Children (SC-UK). These two were among those that regarded slave

traveled to Sudan to redeem slaves to make a journalistic point that slavery exists in Sudan and that in this day and age, one can still purchase slaves for 50 U.S. dollars a piece. AASG got a hold of an escaped Sudanese slave and recruited him as a spokesman for the organization. Francis Bok, a tall, slender, and engaging young Dinka man, toured the United States and gave emotional speeches about his own captivity. He gathered sympathy for the Sudan slaves from rock music concert crowds that AASG enabled him to address and he moved church congregations across the United States. But the most surprising success scored by AASG was in creating the strangest legal bedfellows by getting Johnnie Cochran, the famed OJ Simpson defense attorney, and Kenneth Starr, the special prosecutor in the Clinton-Lewinsky sex scandal, to join hands in defense of two Sudan activists who had been arrested for chaining themselves to the front gate of the Sudan Mission to the United Nations in New York in protest of the Sudan government's use of slavery as a war tactic.

The debate about redemption quickly polarized the opponents of Sudan's slavery into two camps. On one side there were agencies, including the UN and the major human rights groups, that advocated that the focus in the fight against slavery in Sudan should not be on slave redemption but rather on pressuring the very government that perpetrated the practice to desist from it and protect civilians. They suggested the use of diplomatic pressure on the government to end the practice as well as working with it to find ways to release the slaves and punish the culprits. And on the other side there were groups, including AASG, CSI, and a number of other groups and Sudanese diaspora communities, that denounced such a stance as amounting to doing nothing or even direct complicity. Both groups have generally agreed that redemption is not the solution, but the latter group says that engagement with the government of Sudan, a government well known for its intransigence on the slavery issue, without an alternative plan to immediately rescue the abductees is irresponsible. "To sit and do nothing while the slaves rot in captivity until the government has decided to be more humane is negligent if not outright complicit," said one "abolitionist" at a Harvard and Tufts University student demonstration in Boston in 2000. The groups that have supported slave redemption, including a member of the British House of Lords, Baroness Caroline Cox,[1] have all made the point that the current Sudan government, a repressive Islamic extremist regime, has been in

---

[1] Baroness Cox ran a human rights group named Christian Solidarity Worldwide, and has herself made over twenty missions to redeem slaves in south Sudan. When reports of impropriety regarding redemption began to surface, she was much taunted and considered naïve by a number of journalists, a labeling that only increased her resolve to expose the crime of slavery.

were accused in these reports of taking redeemers for a ride by presenting fake slaves for redemption, rounding up some children and women from nearby villages, and presenting them as slaves who had just been brought to the South by Arab middlemen from the north.

These reports have sparked suspicion not just regarding redemption, but about the nature of slavery itself. The fact that there were so many reports about redemption being a hoax, the fact that these slave buy-back missions were not open to independent verifiers, and the tendency among some organizations to inflate the volume of slavery with the assumption that it would earn the slaves more sympathy, have all weakened the position of these antislavery groups. On the one hand the opacity of the process challenged their credibility, and on the other it provided the government of Sudan with room to explain away the entire phenomenon of slavery by arguing that it had come to be an issue in the first place because Western Christian and Zionist zealots and their friends had seized on unproven allegations in order to bring down an Islamic government they would have wanted to bring down anyway. Government agents have seized upon any slight discrepancy in the facts as proof that the whole saga has been a lie all along.

The most convincing argument against slave redemption, however, is the economic one alluded to by UNICEF and Save the Children: that paying for slaves only encourages slave-takers to abduct more in order to sell them back to the redeemers. This point was the subject of a number of journalistic pieces, including a rather well-argued one published in *Atlantic Monthly*. From an empirical perspective there is no evidence that slave redemptions have led to increased raiding, or have increased volume of slaves taken since the programs began. Two factual points need to be illuminated here. One is that slave-raiding is not merely driven by the economics of slavery. Because Sudan's slavery is driven almost solely by its usefulness as a war tactic—to destabilize the support base of the Southern opposition armies by destroying property and displacing the civilian population—it has been able to go on for as long as it has regardless of whether or not redemption happens.

The second point is that redemption had been an ongoing practice since the start of the current wave of slavery in the 1980s, initiated by families to get their loved ones back through their contacts among the Arabs of Darfur and Kordofan, long before the involvement of international groups.

The resurgence of slavery in the early 1980s relates to three main factors. The first is the ethnic, ecological, and economic complexity of the region known as the "transitional zone," where the Dinka and the Baggara share pastures and a major river (Kir) that falls right between the two groups. Both groups' economic activities are tied to a cattle culture, as

agenda of counterinsurgency, as shown by its actions toward the people of the South, is by targeting the family—women and children (Johnson 2002, 157). Such technique is made possible by means of military activities to insure physical disruption of family life through raiding, stripping or destruction of assets, killing of men, and forced relocation of women and children to government-controlled areas. This has been clearly evident, since the start of this round of the war, in Khartoum's attacks on villagers everywhere in the south. These attacks are vicious, aimed at civilians, and are executed either directly by the regular army, through aerial bombardment, or by use of militias recruited from the northern tribal groups hostile to southerners (Christian Aid 2001).

Despite refusal to apply the term "slavery" and referring instead to "abduction," a 1998 UN report admitted for the first time that a large number of women and children were abducted in that year, and were transferred to the areas of the Arab Baggara (UN Commission on Human Rights 1999a). The abduction was carried out by the Baggara-based militia known as the *Murahileen*, which captured these women and children as war booty. This UN report, although a sign of an overdue international recognition of the problem, was a mere scratch on the surface of a much more elaborate government plan of genocide, ethnic mixing, or cultural reconfiguration that targeted the South. The government denied involvement or complicity in slavery but it took no action to halt these practices. But some earlier studies have shown that there were really three different phenomena in the practice of slavery and abduction. First, there was armed and organized raiding in which the role of the government was not clear, and was likely complex. There is information that sometimes the government provided arms, other times the groups of Murahileen went off on their own. Northern tribal groups have been known to organize raids with "representatives" from other Arab groups; returning with children, women, and cattle taken in these raids, all of them have had a common celebration (Jok 2001 and Collins 1992).

Then there was the state-owned military supply train escorted by the Popular Defense Forces (PDF) which traveled slowly from the north down through contested territory of Aweil and Wau in Bahr el-Ghazal. It is evident that there was formal recruitment by the government of militias to guard the train from possible SPLA attacks. These Murahileen (or *Mujahideen*, holy warriors, as they were sometimes called) then went out from the train and attacked villages suspected of supporting the SPLA on the way from Babanusa to Wau and back. According to eyewitness accounts that we have received over the years, the Murahileen used to ride on horseback along both sides of the railroad tracks, fanning out to a radius of up to 50 km, and systematically raided villages, torched houses, stole cattle, and killed men who put up any resistance. Their booty consisted not

that these wars were responsible for nearly half of the 4.5 million internally displaced persons (IDPs) in Sudan. Among the displacements due to slave raiding, estimates have put the Dinka of Aweil IDP population at 200,000 civilians, with the death of thousands more in the period between 1998 and 2001 alone (CARE International 2001). The raids have caused disruption of Dinka economic activity as well as relief services such as child immunization campaigns and feeding programs for undernourished children. On the other hand, where the government of Sudan did not encounter major SPLA military resistance, their rapidly growing ascendancy became clear. Here the military situation was ominous in the extreme for the civilian populations. In an extension of the scorched-earth tactics that created displacement of populations throughout the transitional zone since 1983, Sudan gained the reputation of being the country with the world's largest internally displaced population.

Although a tense debate over Sudan's slavery has gone on for over two decades, such a debate has been over the volume, the causes, who benefits from it, or how to stop it; there has been little doubt that slavery exists. One important development that has helped put that doubt to rest is the return of a number of Dinka children from captivity. These children had been in bondage for some time, and were able to return either through escape or redemption. The redemption was the result of long-standing efforts by Dinka families to locate and return their children from enslavement. By the time international redemption groups became involved in the mid-1990s, redemptions had been going on since the start of the current wave of slavery in the 1980s, initiated by families to get their loved ones back through their contacts among the Arabs of Darfur and Kordofan. Redemption had operated on the basis that a Dinka family would sell some of their belongings, usually cattle, and seek an Arab intermediary; trace the whereabouts of their abductees, and initiate a negotiation with the abductor or the current holder and settle on the price; the abductees would be released to the intermediary, who in turn guided the abductees back to their families. Although it had gone on for a long time, this was a limited-scale operation because people could not afford the cost, and so when antislavery groups found out about it, they began to support many more families to secure the freedom and return of their members through these clandestine channels. This support surely went a long way for the families who gained the freedom of their members without incurring too much expense in terms of property. When more and more people began to be released through these channels, more money began to pour in, and with more money coming into the small cash-poor economy of south Sudan, the local authorities began to get involved, which initially meant nominal taxes levied on the incoming foreign currency through control of the exchange rate. More slaves bought

details of raids, names of authority figures, names of people killed, estimates of property destroyed, and the names of abductees, including their gender, their identifying clan, and the name of the village or cattle camp from which they were abducted. This registry, although not complete, has generated a database that looks like a missing persons report, and has 12 thousand abductees in it—not estimates, but real people with real names whose relatives are known. This database will assist in tracing and reunification, should the political situation becomes amenable to such an exercise. But beyond this, the database dispels without a shred of a doubt the question about the existence of slavery and other gruesome rights violations. It has to be noted that enslavement is only the sharp end of a long process of violent activities, starting with an attack on a village, burning of property, killing of those trying to defend the village, and chaining and dragging of captives across the rough terrain between the south and the north. So, long before the fate of the abductees is decided by the captors, and long before the much-debated redemption becomes an issue, there are a host of rights violations that are worthy of their own attention.

Addendum

During my trip to south Sudan in the summer of 2004 it was clear that the abduction issue was subordinated to the hopes for peace, and there seem to be a desire, among both the officials of the SPLA and some of the chiefs, to focus on the future rather than push for restoration of justice to the victims of abduction and slavery. It is surprising that this nonchalant attitude about the right of the victims to assistance to return home or for compensation is happening in an environment where the families of the victims, some former slaves, and the international human rights circles are discussing how measures of such restoration of justice could be built into the peace process. Apparently, because these voices are calling upon the international community, especially on the mediating governments in the peace process, to have abduction and slavery addressed at the peace talks, there is an increasing fear in Khartoum that evidence of the government's involvement in abduction and slavery might become clear when a peace deal is reached and an open investigation into these crimes may finally be conducted. This fear is especially intense because of the failures of CEAWAC to achieve its goals. CEAWAC had been set up to paint a picture that the government is working to end abduction, compensate the victims, and facilitate the release and return of the abductees. The funds for CEAWAC operations had been provided by UNICEF, and expertise in child protection issues was provided by Save the Children. But at the conditions of the returned abductees were so incredibly pitiful that the main welfare agencies operating in the area such as UNICEF and Save Children refused to be part of this operation.

We were told that these agencies had disagreed with the manner in which the operation was conducted. There was no adequate coordination with the agencies or with the local authorities. There were no systems in place to speed up a process of unifying the returning abductees with their families upon arrival. The agencies felt that the whole operation was not done right. No provisions for the protection of child rights were made. There was no proper investigation of the status of individuals to ascertain whether they were abductees or IDPs of another kind. There were no proper interviews conducted with the abductees to insure their willingness to return to the south. No measures of care were set up in the receiving locations prior to their return so that proper reception was set up beforehand.

The result was that when the abductees were returned and "dumped" (as the abductees describe their return) in the south, this was done without basic services being provided. No provisions were made to feed them during the time it would take to find family members, not to mention the lack of clean drinking water, cooking utensils, water containers, shelter, and other basic needs. This was especially deplorable considering that identification and reunification was not an immediate process, the original home villages of the abductees were not identified beforehand, which meant that some abductees were returned to areas so distant from their own villages that no one among the host communities could recognize them. This situation became much harder in the case of people who may have been abducted at a young age and could not be clear about their families, clans, figures of authority, or names of villages. Many such people were still stranded in the camps at the time of our visit in July 2004, and the possibility of ever finding their relatives is next to nil, especially since no one is actively looking into their cases. We met and interviewed a few such boys in Alek in Gogrial county. Some of them speak of a return to the north. Indeed, a few have reportedly already returned to the north.

Given that they had been rounded up without insuring the consent of the abductees, the international welfare agencies such as UNICEF refused to get involved in the care of them. However, CEAWAC and the SPLM authorities in Bahr el-Ghazal had agreed that CEAWAC would set up a camp and provide services for one month, during which tracing of relatives and reunification would take place. But such services were not provided, and much suffering ensued. Throughout the summer of 2004 some women and children died of starvation, and two women gave birth in open air. Some field staff from other agencies whom we interviewed

agreement nor provisions to look after them or integrate them into their communities.

Because of this experience, many people, among both the returnees and the local population, say that the official line was hard to believe because of the apparent lack of interest among the local staff about "returning our people." People were particularly unhappy with the way the local authorities did not seem to be bothered by this "dumping," to use their word. The returning abductees themselves spoke of having been abducted again from the north and forced to come back to the south.

Bibliography

CARE International (2001), *Internal Displacement: Causes and Remedies*. Atlanta: CARE International.

Christian Aid (2001), *The Scorched Earth: Oil and War in the Sudan*. London: Christian Aid.

Collins, Robert (1992), "Nilotic Slavery: Past and Present," in Elizabeth Savage (ed.), *Human Commodity* (London: Frank Cass), pp. 210–231.

Deng, Francis M. (1995), *War of Visions*. Washington, DC: Brookings Institution.

Harker, John (2000), *Human Security in Sudan: The Report of a Canadian Assessment Mission* (part 1). Prepared for the Minister of Foreign Affairs, Ottawa.

Hendrie, B. et al., eds. (1996), *Operation Lifeline Sudan: A Review* (independent consultant report).

Human Rights Watch (HRW) (1999), *World Report: Events of December 1997–November 1998*. Washington, DC: HRW.

Johnson, Douglas (2003), *The Root Causes of Sudan's Civil Wars*. Oxford: James Currey.

Jok, Jok Madut (2001), *War and Slavery in Sudan*. Philadelphia: University of Pennsylvania Press.

Jok, Jok Madut (2004), "The Targeting of Civilians as Military Tactics" in Ann Lesch and Osman Fadl (eds.), *Coping with Torture: Images from the Sudan* (Trenton, NJ and Asmara: Red Sea Press).

UN Commission on Human Rights (1998), *Report of the Special Rapporteur on the Situation of Human Rights in the Sudan*. Geneva: Document E/CN.4/1998/66.

UN Commission on Human Rights (CHR) (1999a), *Question of the Violation of Human Rights and Fundamental Freedoms in Any Part of the World: Situation of Human Rights in the Sudan*, E/CN.4/1999/38/Add.1.

UN Commission on Human Rights (CHR) (1999b), *Situation of Human Rights in Sudan: Visit of the Special Rapporteur Mr. Leornardo Franco*, 13–24 February 1999, Addendum to E/CN.4/1999/38.

UN General Assembly (UN GA) (2000), *Human Rights Questions: Human Rights Situations and Reports of Special Rapporteurs and Representatives: Situation of Human Rights in the Sudan*, A/55/374.

Introduction

On the eve of independence in most of French West Africa, it was reported that slavery still existed and that slaves were still being bought
and sold.[1] The British and Foreign Anti-Slavery Society undertook to assess for itself this horrific legacy of colonialism. Timbuktu, once an obses-
sion for European travelers who willingly gave their lives in the quest to
"discover" it, became newly infamous as a place where anyone—even a
European—could buy a slave. Robin Maugham's *Slaves of Timbuktu*
(1961) showed that it was also a place where Europeans could still buy
freedom for Africans.[2] Both concepts, buying a slave and buying freedom, were anathema to postwar Europe. Maugham expressed unease at
his venture—purchasing the freedom of one slave in order to prove the
continued traffic in so many others. But this was less because of any
moral reflection on the inherent contradiction in the process than guilt
that he was misleading the local commandant, who treated him well
(1961, 204–205). Maugham's aim was to shock his benefactors and
those who would support the Society into "abolitionist action" with
his stories of contemporary slavery, cruelty, and slave-marketing. But his
achievement from an historian's perspective was to reveal, through his
various interviews with slaves, slave masters, and "freed" slaves, the
complexity of the issues surrounding the whole question of "slave
redemption."

The selection of quotations with which this chapter is introduced suggests a number of those issues, including some implicit contradictions.
On the one hand, it seems that being "freed" did not necessarily mean
being "free," and that to whatever degree it did, it was dependent on
freedom being obtained in a particular way. Both descriptions of (former)
slave and (former) slave master seem to be assuming a common Muslim
identity, the former indirectly with the reference to being a "slave in his
heart," the latter directly with the statement that he has "only sold a
slave." The former could realize "freedom" only if he purchased it himself; the latter could realize being a good Muslim only if he personally
"freed" the slave. On the other hand, the three quotations attributed to
local free/freedmen all raise the specter of the French as cultural and political interlopers, whose role as "abolitionists" is at best ambivalent. If
when the French left, it was believed by slaves and masters alike that
a master could (and would) retake his slaves, then clearly "law" had

---

[1] *Rapport des Nations Unis sur l'esclavage*, 1950 (Archives Nationales du Sénégal, AOF.
2K15 174 Mauritanie).

[2] The process of purchasing a slave is recounted in detail in Maugham (1961), pp. 201–204.

thereof) among Africans involved. Others in this collection are addressing the situation in Sudan, where "slave sales" in recent years have already provoked considerable international controversy. I would like to turn to the other "villain" in the region, Mauritania, where efforts of redemption societies like Christian Solidarity International have not yet manifested themselves in spite of ongoing reports of slavery and slave sales.[5]

Colonialism and *Rachat:* The Buying of Freedom

The Islamic Republic of Mauritania was created by policy that reflected French concerns for French West Africa (AOF) more generally; it was also carved out of a Sahara that generated policies unique to the desert and encompassed part of southern Morocco and eastern/central Mali (home to Timbuktu's Tuaregs). This ambiguous position was well reflected in the evolution of French policy regarding slaves and *rachat*—"buying back." The first thing to make clear is that French concern to end slavery—or more specifically, to end it for African masters—was nothing new when Maugham encountered it in the 1950s. On the contrary, it echoed policies dating to the initial French conquest of West Africa in the 1880s and 1890s. The establishment of *villages de liberté* or "liberty villages" was envisaged to provide refuge for slaves seeking escape from masters; the villages were also intended to absorb slaves the French administration "taxed" (as they taxed all goods in kind) from caravans passing by their scattered frontier customs posts. Once registered as residents of these villages, these slaves were to be given "liberty." However, the villages were provided with almost no resources (including land), and by dint of their location near railheads and administration posts, they served largely as labor reserves. Slaves who registered worked for a three-month period, during which time they could be reclaimed by masters. They could also be hired out, with arrangements made for part of their salary to be put towards their "price of liberation." Initially, that price was some Fr 300, a price well above the cost of "slave replacement" and certainly well beyond what any wages could accommodate. (In the late 1890s, the price was reduced to Fr 200.) At the same time, masters could also claim up to Fr 1 per day of their slave's wages (presumably, before reclaiming them); few slaves were actually paid more than that.

[5] The national antislavery society working actively to bring slavery and slaves to the attention of international audiences is SOS Esclaves Mauritanie. An internet search reveals the extent to which it has been successful in disseminating information; its 2001–03 reports are available at http://sos.iabolish.com/report-2001-French.rtf; http://sos.iabolish.com/SOS-Report-2003-French.rtf.

Fr 100 on average per *rachat* and that in some areas, traders refused to do business with them. Moreover, whether buying from local communities or slave merchants, this price could only purchase the old, the sick, and those ostracized for crimes like sorcery or intended as part of funerary sacrifices; often they were children—usually in poor health, already abandoned (Bouche 1968, 192, 255). "It was rare that missions were presented with well-constituted children: their masters knew that they could get much more profit elsewhere, anywhere from Fr 180, 200 to 300" (Bouche 1968, 194). If in principle the acquired freedom of any slave should have been equal to the freedom of any other in the battle to end slavery (and populate villages), what is clear from these complaints is that missionaries' zeal for slave redemption was tied to their recognition that the Christianizing of Africa was rooted in *rachat*. The missionaries' very *raison d'être* was reflected in these pitiful, purchased slaves; they were not yet ready to admit that these might not prove suitable pillars of faith (Bouche 1968, 194).

Soon these villages, like those of the administration, began to attract refugees in search of food and sustenance during times of drought or famine. But like slaves who were excessively expensive, these refugees too were often turned away (Klein 1998, 117). Reports of these instances and ongoing complaints from the missions about inadequate resources gained an ear in France. The Anti-Slavery Society committed itself to fundraising for slave purchases. There were several schemes proposed in letters and advertisements in the society's *Journal*. It was suggested that "liberty villages" be named after donors who contributed funds for purchasing slave residents; in 1896 one prominent cardinal wondered publicly if prospective donors might not be attracted by the possibility of naming newly purchased children. The White Father's *Bulletin* similarly suggested that donors contributing at least the price of one slave (that is, Fr 100) should be permitted to give the baptismal name; to be permitted to name a whole village would be "even more glorious." In the 1902 edition of the Anti-Slavery Society's journal the priest of one of Paris's most populous parishes proposed raising Fr 6000 among parishioners to create a new village that would carry the name of their patron saint, Saint Joseph. And an elderly woman proposed sending Fr 6000 to establish a village in the name of a dear, deceased friend; she expressed the hope to be able to do the same for herself, before she died (Bouche 1968, 184–185).

It is clear that *rachat*, the idea of "slave redemption," had as fully captured Catholic imagination as it had colonial policy; but it is also clear from the failure to follow through on most of these proposals that the goal of creating free Christian souls was no more capable of generating resources than the goal of creating "free" marketplace workers. "Liberty" was conspicuously absent from the "villages" to which its name

understood by the local populations who honestly return the fugitives, exchanging them for goods with the Mission. . . . The *villages de liberté* (or the Christian villages formed by purchased slaves) permitted the missionaries to install themselves in a 'slave milieu,' to be accepted there, to endure" (Bouche 1968, 255).

The missions sometimes sought to purchase the "freedom" of relatives of their converts or workers and they were known to put pressure on masters to set a modest ransom for these special cases. They also took in many "pawns"—though it was often unclear to local people whether they were giving refuge or actually purchasing them. Pawning was an important survival strategy in both the Sahara and the Sahel. "Pawns," usually children, were used to help pay off debts, the intent being to redeem them when the debt and its interest was covered. They were also used in times of great difficulty, like the droughts and famines that hit these regions periodically. Children of working age would be exchanged for a sum of money; they would be assured food and lodging, and the rest of the family could use the money to buy themselves the same. The aim was for the family to repay the "loan" in better times and recoup the pawn. In reality, the interest levied on the loan often necessitated leaving the child indefinitely with the debtor—essentially as a very cheap slave. When missions took in or "bought" pawns, then, it was seen as exactly that: a means of obtaining very cheap labor. They were acting just as a wealthy merchant or powerful family might act in the village or clan. Indeed, as the missions "inserted themselves" in these *sociétés esclavagistes*, they were accepted largely because they took on such a role. While they may have convinced themselves that they were rescuing slaves, masters simply saw them as relieving their own burden in difficult times: increasingly, they would turn their slaves loose to seek refuge at the missions, or offer their slave children as pawns—then return to reclaim them later (Klein 1998, 117).

Consequently, far from "ending slavery" by buying freedom, French policies and practices (broadly defined to include the secular and religious) reshaped slavery by buying more slaves. The impact was not so much felt through the "market," as no form of *rachat* ever seems to have been at high enough prices to encourage expanding supply or even significantly raising profits. It was felt more at a social level, where French administrators and French missionaries created a role for themselves—or perhaps more accurately, had that role created for them, that was, for the most part, compatible with local cultural customs. Buying slaves was . . . buying slaves. Using slaves for labor was . . . using slave labor. Doing both was . . . becoming a master. Negotiating with masters was . . . acknowledging masters' authority and responsibility. African or European, authority was authority. It really did not matter.

women and children between army officers and soldiers (many of whom were African) and local African notables and interpreters lived on in the twentieth-century Mauritanian practice of providing locally based *tirailleurs* with "slave" wives. Soon "marriages" that were little more than slave prostitution prompted the authorities to insist that the slave woman be purchased before the marriage. Then fears that these wives would in fact be re-enslaved when they returned to Senegal or Mali with their husbands led to a prohibition on taking Mauritanian wives out of the colony. Children of these marriages, on the other hand, were a different issue: *tirailleurs* could claim and take children as long as it could be proven they had been born within wedlock—otherwise, they were regarded as slaves belonging to the (former) master of the woman/wife (McDougall 1988, 370–371). These rather bizarre regulations reflected an interesting attempt by the French colonial authorities to respect several not necessarily compatible sets of values: patriarchy and marriage as defined by French law and culture; Islam and slavery as defined by Mauritanian law and custom; colonialism and abolition as defined by French policy and practice. The mix saw cases spanning ten or more years as family members fought over inherited slaves, husbands and masters fought over "wives," and everyone fought over children. Women seldom won (unless they were also "masters"—and a significant number were), children were never asked. The most vulnerable became even more so thanks to *rachat* and abolition. Masters often accepted "payment" for female slaves: they called it bride price for a woman still enslaved, the French called it "purchase" of a woman now "free." Meanwhile *tirailleurs* enjoyed (exploited) what were essentially concubines until they left Mauritania; if they were lucky they also got children out of the deal. Masters who exploited both Islamic law and French policy generally retained their female slaves in the end, having been compensated handsomely for their temporary absence. Local administrators found themselves mired in the middle, often for a very long time.

That this situation still pertained in 1950 drew international attention. Indeed, this was the backdrop against which the British and Foreign Anti-Slavery Society launched several investigations of its own, one being the excursion by Robin Maugham to Timbuktu that we encountered at the outset of this chapter. Another had taken place just two years earlier, this one to Morocco and Mauritania. Or, more precisely, to Morocco—permission was never granted for the investigators to enter Mauritania. Consequently, they sought sources in the southern Moroccan town of Goulimine that could shed light on slavery to the south (Fox-Pitt 1957, 19–20, 25). And they found them. Commander T. Fox-Pitt published findings in the *Anti-Slavery Reporter* in 1957 that included two "testimonies" of former slaves (26, 27). These are clearly problematic from a

escaped I went to the French at their office in the town of Atar. They held me until my master arrived and then they handed me back to him. I was beaten with a camel whip called a *cravache*. My master made a hole in the lobe of my ear. . . . He put a thong through this and led me with my hands tied behind my back walking beside him as he rode a camel. This is how I was taken back to his camp. I wore nothing but rags when I was a slave. I looked after the camels. *Later I made a successful escape from slavery. I now live free and well in Goulimine. I have food and clothes and work to do and lead a prosperous life.* My father escaped from slavery before me and my mother is dead, so I was able to leave without leaving anyone behind. I came alone.

Rachat from a Slave's Perspective

Ould Ahmed Aida's slave draws our attention to the now familiar but still ambiguous policy of the colonial rulers "buying the freedom of slaves." On the one hand, he recounted that he (and the other slaves) were "forcibly" removed from their master when the latter moved into town, on the other, that this same master was paid the price of Fr 20,000. First they were "freed," and then they were "imprisoned" and forced to work. Then, they were beaten and our informant ran away, back to his master. Contradictory though these descriptions seem, they are not inconsistent with the historical experience of *rachat* as we have come to understand it—or more importantly, as the former slave himself understood it. He was "purchased" by the French and told he was free. The administration's policy of having slaves "work off" their redemption (thereby keeping them from that feared "theft and vagabondage" which lack of resources would induce, while simultaneously getting work done) was "prison" and "forced labor" to bin M'barak. So, if he was not going to be "free" in any meaningful sense, he would rather return to his master— whom he clearly continued to think of as "his master"—and be a slave. The fact that he did not comment on a return to slavery *per se* suggests that at best he had seen himself as "freed" by the French, not as "free." He spoke of returning to his master as returning from his "new master," the French, to his "old one," Emir ould Ahmed Aida. It is consistent with a belief on his part—as well as his master's—that he was still a slave; consequently, it was natural to then speak of Caid Dahmane buying him (for the second time), "to set him at liberty."

Caid Dahmane ould Beyrouk ould Abidine, mayor of Goulimine, generously purchased bin M'barak from his master for Fr 50,000 (according to his own testimony, also recorded by Fox-Pitt [1957, 26]). This of course is in stark contrast to the *rachat* (of Fr 20,000) reported by bin

"Abide El Barka . . ." to "El Barka." He explained that *abide* was the plural of *abd*, meaning slave "and not correctly part of a name" (1957, 27). Other evidence from Goulimine would suggest the meaning, if not the name itself, did indeed apply; and it is not impossible that he was literally referred to in this way. "Slave of el-Barka," which was what the name meant, could well pertain—he was 'bin M'Barak, son of M'Barak, among the slaves of Barka. This raises a rather interesting possibility: Fatma's master and Dahmane's son-in-law was Mohamed Barka. Just a year before her death, Fatma received her first ever "national identity card." She had given her legal name as "Faytma Barka" (McDougall 1998, 305). Had bin M'Barak also been "a slave of Barka" following on his arrival in Goulimine? Was his "free" life as a mason akin to Fatma's life as a bread seller (and also, at one stage, a sardine-canning factory worker [288, 289])? If this was the case, there is no question that "free" meant "freed"—*haratin* in the Mauritanian sense (see below), even if he himself did not use the term.

M'Barjarek bin Bilal ("son of Bilal," the black slave of the prophet Mohamed, affirming his inherited slave status) recounted an equally re-vealing, if more suspect, biography. His account of being punished and returned to his master as a fugitive slave is consistent with early French policy; it is perhaps less clear that he would have been so readily returned to his master in the 1950s. But it is possible. However, as an escaped slave arriving in Goulimine, supposedly alone on a camel (which he would have had to have stolen from his master's herd), he would have had no choice but to seek out a *patron* from one of the leading families. As it happens, we know his master "Hamidi" had commercial dealings with the merchants of Goulimine at this time, including the Beyrouk (Mc-Dougall 1988, 381).[6] There is no way that one of his known slaves would have been permitted to claim both his own freedom and the value of the camel without someone, quite probably the Beyrouk themselves, paying a price. A *hartani* experience comparable to that of Fatma, Messoud, and (probably) bin M'Barak was more likely to have provided the "food, clothing, and work" he enjoyed. Food, clothing, work—the essence of both slavery and freed-slavery. And also, apparently "freedom."

[6] The article says "Morocco"; my oral interview work subsequently in Goulimine (sev-eral occasions between 1993 and 1996), with "Hamidi's" son Mohamed Said ould Hamody (2000, Washington, DC) and most recently with several *haratine* related to Hamody's family confirms the Goulimine-Beyrouk connection. Hamody frequently sent camels north with his *haratine* in order to bring back Moroccan merchandise. Two promi-nent Beyruk cousins also established themselves in Atar. Relations between Hamody and the Beyruk family included marital and "milk-kin"; there were also relations between their respective slaves. Both sets of relations are being explored further as part of my current work on the Hamody family.

ability—to buy slaves affirmed the difference between being freed and being slave (1988, 382–384). Bin Bilal's testimony confirms this to have been the case, at least from his perspective. If ownership of slaves was not the prerogative of the free, freedom was not the antithesis of slavery. Not, at least, in Mauritania. In short, the cast of characters in these Goulimine vignettes that supposedly vilify Mauritania and the French while acknowledging the progress and humanitarianism of Goulimine—where, according to Caid Dahmane and bin Bilal, so many Mauritanian slaves sought refuge from the *cravache*—generates nothing but continued questions, not about what slavery was, but about what freedom was not.

These testimonies, the odd anecdote (often unattributed), some recent interviews with former slaves—they are not enough to give us the extensive "slave perspective" we truly need here. However, they are enough from which to argue that the issues are complex ones, varying from person to person, from region to region (and, I would argue, from men to women). One anecdote (repeated in a 1912 publication to explain why the *village* policy failed) cited an anonymous "liberated slave" from one of the villages as responding to the question "how are conditions?" with the complaint that "they had no slaves to help them in the fields" (Bouche 1968, 159). The acceptance of "slavery" as a social and economic reality continued even among those who had been enslaved. This anecdote from the era of the *villages de libérté* may be apocryphal or perhaps exceptional—but Hamody was neither. Not only did slaves who had been freed accept the concept of slavery, they embraced using slave labor to better their own position, and owning slave "people" to reinforce their own social distance from slavery. Because the issue was not "freedom" versus "slavery" but rather "freed" versus "non-freed," the acquisition of rights to slave labor or slave ownership affirmed one's "non-slave" status.

There were other issues as well, as Fatma's story in particular illuminates. Fatma was Muslim. Her telling of her tale emphasized several details about how important her slave status was to her Islamic one. Among references to the pious nature of her master—in a sense, a kind of "mirror" to her own—was the insistence that she was not his daughter (although she'd arrived with him in Goulimine as a child) but that he had bought her. She was his slave. This statement was repeated at least twice in a context that to me seemed not to warrant this specificity. On the contrary, if she could have been mistaken for his daughter (she was Malian, but so was her master's wife at the time), would she not have wanted that to be the case (McDougall 1998, 300–301)? It was only after her death, when I found out that she had been Mohamed Barka's concubine, that I understood: in Islam, concubinage is completely acceptable. Honourable, even. However, only slaves can be concubines. It is forbidden to take free

The fact here is that it was not the *purchase price* that brought true free-dom for the slave, it was the *pilgrimage:* one could redeem oneself with money; legal freedom did not necessitate the *hajj*. But one could *not* make the *hajj* without being legally free. It was in this act that Islam and Freedom intersected, and one came to define the other.

To return full circle to Robin Maugham's experience in Timbuktu in the late 1950s and to the quotations with which we began this explo-ration, it was clear that Islam, "faith," shaped masters' and slaves' views of each other and of their world. The Tuareg master who sold his slave apparently had second thoughts about the relative gain he had made: he was no longer certain that the money he had received was worth the blessing he had lost by selling rather than freeing the man.[12] From the slave's perspective, the explanation given Maugham as to why a slave would not just ask for his freedom, namely that he would know he was a slave in his heart unless and until he had properly purchased his own freedom, was another way of expressing the same Islamic beliefs as those held by the slave from Saint Louis. Similarly, another slave Maugham met in Timbuktu had been "released" many years before by his master to fend for himself. Now growing watermelons for a living, he still paid his master (and he called him that) an annual "head tax"; in good years he gave him an extra "present." "I still belong to my master" the man said, "and so do my four children. I know that the law today prevents my mas-ter from forcing my sons to go back to him. But if my master sent for them they would feel bound to go, for they know they are his slaves" (Maugham 1961, 169). Maugham also met a former slave who re-counted a situation in which it was his master who reaffirmed "tradi-tional" Muslim beliefs and custom, albeit in a less than benevolent fash-ion. The slave told Maugham that back in the 1930s, he had left his master and joined his runaway slave parents in Timbuktu. There, with his father's help, he had received the support of the commandant to re-main, ostensibly, "free." His master had soon arrived to take him back, and the commandant had intervened, telling his master that under French law he was free. His master had sought time alone with him and essen-tially threatened him with continual harassment and possible re-enslave-ment if and when the French ever left—unless, that is, he *bought* his own liberty according to a price he, the master, would fix, in which case he would be "free" for good. "So I saved every franc I could. And at last

---

[12] This point was made repeatedly by people I interviewed from Hamody's immediate and "extended" (*hartani*) family: to sell your slaves was "*honte*"—shame. One would sell almost anything—animals, houses, land—before selling a slave. The fact that so many were sold to Hamody in the 1940s in particular, and that people sought him out to buy their slaves, underscores the economic penury experienced by the region at this time.

three central observations, all articulated in the opening quotations. To be freed is not necessarily to be free, to speak of cultural context is to speak of historical experience, to see Islam only as the property of the master is to miss the essence of being slave and Muslim. Or perhaps I hoped to do slightly more. Perhaps I hoped that echoes might resonate around the morality of "buying slaves," whatever the end purpose, however Christian the process. The idea that one culture's vision of what slavery is, and who slaves are, can effectively illuminate another culture's history; the claim that there is "nothing political" in the act of chronicling, let along "ending," slavery; the naivety we share in our belief that not only do we know best, we can do no harm—to all of the above, history has a lot to say, if we take the time to listen.

Bibliography

Books and Articles

Bouche, Denise (1968), *Les Villages de liberté en Afrique noire française 1887–1910*. Paris: Mouton & Co. and Ecole Pratique des Hautes Etudes.

Fox-Pitt, Com. T. (1957), "Report of an Investigation in Morocco in October and November, 1956," *The Anti-Slavery Reporter and Aborigines' Friend* 11(1): 19–27.

Klein, Martin (1998), *Slavery and Colonial Rule in French West Africa*. Cambridge: Cambridge University Press.

Maugham, Robin (1961), *Slaves of Timbuktu*. London: Longmans. Green and Co. Inc.

McDougall, E. Ann (1988), "Topsy-Turvy World: Slaves and Freed Slaves in the Mauritanian Adrar, 1910–1950," in R. Roberts and S. Miers (eds.), *The Ending of Slavery in Africa* (Madison: University of Wisconsin Press), pp. 362–388.

McDougall, E. Ann (1998), "Islam: an overview," in Paul Finkleman and Joseph C. Miller (eds.), *Encyclopedia of World Slavery* (New York: Macmillan Reference), vol. 1, pp. 434–439.

McDougall, E. Ann (2000), "'A Quest for Honour': Islam, Slavery and the Contributions of Martin Klein to African History," in Richard Roberts and Philip Zachernuk, "On Slavery and Islam in African History: A tribute to Martin Klein," special edition of the *Canadian Journal of African Studies* 34(3): 546–564.

McDougall, E. Ann, Mesky Brhane, and Urs Peter Ruf (2003), "Legacy of Slavery; Promise of Democracy: Mauritania in the 21st Century," in Malinda Smith (ed.), *Globalizing Africa* (New Jersey: Africa World Press), pp. 67–88.

McDougall, E. Ann, and Mohamed Hassan Mohamed (1999), "Les Maisons Beyrouk et Illigh: Construction d' identité au Maroc de Sud, 16éme a 18éme siécles," paper presented at the second Table Ronde de Goulimine, conference jointly sponsored Centre National de Recherche Scientifique, Paris and Institut de Recherche Scientifique, Rabat, Morocco, February 1999 (unpublished).

Part III

HISTORICAL CONSIDERATIONS

Chapter Eight

The End of Serfdom in Russia—Lessons for Sudan?

LISA D. COOK

The literature on slavery in the Americas is often cited when the current problem of slavery in Sudan is considered. But in addition to looking to American slavery as a benchmark, it would be equally instructive to examine the less-compared serf-emancipation schemes developed and executed by tsarist Russia. Emancipation and redemption schemes have been debated and, with some controversy and mixed success, implemented in Sudan. Elaboration of the factors influencing design of an abolition program may shed light on alternatives available to those considering emancipation in Sudan.

The Mechanics of Serfdom in Russia

Serfdom comprised a number of forms of limited (by law or by custom) ownership of human beings or legal claims to varying parts of their wealth, income, or services.[1] A serf and the serfowner's land were typically an asset bundle, and title to the land included title to the serf.

Data on the evolution of serfdom, on serfs during the eighteenth and nineteenth centuries, and on serfs and serfowners on the eve of emancipation reported in tables 8.1, 8.2, and 8.3 may be useful in understanding the timing, scale, and scope of serfdom in Russia. Blum's (1961) estimates of the number and proportion of male serfs in the Russian population are given in table 8.2. While most series suggest a decline in the proportion of serfs between 1800 and 1861, estimates vary. The estimates of Hoch and Augustine (2001), for example, are generally lower than Blum's. They estimate that 50.1 percent of the male population was enserfed in 1811, and that this fell to 36.5 percent by 1857.

---

[1] See Kahan (1973) for a fuller discussion of the definition of serfdom and Troinitskii (1861) for a summary of the rights and responsibilities of serfs and serfowners.

TABLE 8.1 *(Continued)*

1858	Main Committee on the Peasant Question replaces Secret Committee; prepares first abolition program based on the Lithuanian rescript but does not initially guarantee freed serfs land
	Wave of disturbances in Estonia after 1856 decree (above) published
	Alexander II tours provinces
1859	Alexander II approves creation of the Editing Commissions to draft statutes abolishing serfdom
1861	*Alexander II signs into law the Proclamation and Statutes abolishing serfdom*
	Massacres of peasants protesting terms of reform in Kandeevka, Penza, Bezdna, Kazan provinces
	Peace mediators begin to arrive in villages to oversee implementation of reform
1863	Formal start of "Temporary Obligation"
	Polish nationalist revolt, terms of abolition changed by Russian government in favor of peasants
	Reform of appanage peasants across Russian Empire; could redeem land after 1865
1866	Reform of state peasants; transferred to equivalent of "temporary obligation"
1881	*Alexander III succeeds to the throne*
	Transfer to redemption required for all peasants still in "temporary obligation" from 1883; redemption payments and compensation to nobles lowered
1883–87	Abolition of poll tax in European provinces of the Russian Empire
1886	State peasants permitted to redeem their land
1894	*Nicholas II succeeds to the throne*
1905	*Outbreak of Revolution*
	Announcement of end of redemption payments, effective January 1, 1907
1906	Peasants granted freedom of movement; peasant households permitted to leave village communes
1907	*End of Redemption Operation*

Source: Moon (2001).
Note: Author's emphasis.

In 1859 and throughout the history of serfdom in Russia generally, *pomeshchik* serfs dominated the serf population and, among them, peasants assigned to settled lands constituted the majority, or 93 percent, of *pomeshchik* serfs.[2] These peasants were required to work three days a week for the *pomeshchiki* in order to fulfill their principal duty, which

---

[2] A *pomeshchik* is a noble landowner. Only hereditary gentry and *pomeshchiki* could own serfs. This exposition relies heavily on Troinitskii (1861).

TABLE 8.3
Serf and Serfowner Population in Russia, 1859

(A)

Serfs	Total	Share
Pomeshchik serfs	22,284,876	0.97
Male	10,858,357	0.47
Female	11,426,519	0.50
Peasants, various departments	242,156	0.01
Male	127,101	0.01
Female	115,055	0.00
Mill and factory	542,599	0.02
Male	259,455	0.01
Female	283,144	0.01
Total	*23,069,631*	*1.00*

(B)

Serfowners	Total	Number Male Serfs Owned	Share Serfowners by Category
Landless gentry	3,633	12,045	0.03
Pomeshchiks holding:	100,247	10,539,137	0.97
up to 21 serfs	41,016	327,534	0.39
21 to 100 serfs	35,498	1,666,073	0.34
101 to 500 serfs	19,930	3,925,102	0.19
501 to 1000 serfs	2,421	1,569,888	0.02
>1000 serfs	1,382	3,050,540	0.01
Total	*103,880*	*10,551,182*	*1.00*

(C)

Total inhabitants of the Empire	64,081,167
Serf population, percent total	34.39
Serfowner population, percent total	0.16
Average serf/serfowner ratio, males	101.57
Average serf/serfowner ratio, all *pomeshchik*	222.30

Source: 10th Revision, Russian National Census as reported in Troinitskii (1861); author's calculations.

Note: Data in panel (A) are for European Russia, Siberia, and the Transcaucasian krai. Data in panel (B) are for European Russia.

clothing, and state taxes. Seventy-six percent of *pomeshchik* serfowners held 100 or fewer serfs. Three percent of *pomeshchik* serfowners held more than 500 serfs. Regions and provinces varied widely in the proportion of serf population. More than one third of provinces and *oblasts* in European Russia and the Transcaucasus had serf populations of greater than

TABLE 8.5
Serfs' State and Seigniorial Obligations, Male Serfs, 1700–99

	STATE OBLIGATIONS			SEIGNIORIAL OBLIGATIONS						
	Direct Taxes			Dues (obrok)			Labor (barshchina)			
								Value of harvest		Index of
Years	Roubles	Index A	Index B	Roubles	Index A	Index B	Area, desiatinii	Index A	Index B	Grain Prices
1700–09	0.27	100	100	0.40	100	100	0.60	100	100	100
1710–19	0.70	259	96	0.50	125	69				180
1720–29	0.70	259	115	0.70	175	67				263
1730–39	0.70	259	94	0.90	225	100				226
1740–49	0.70	259	103	1.20	300	108				277
1750–59	0.70	259	72	1.60	400	159				251
1760–69	0.70	259	58	3.00	750	207	0.75	452	125	362
1770–79	0.70	259	37	4.50	1125	253	1.20	1130	200	444
1780–89	0.70	259	32	6.00	1500	219				686
1790–99	0.96	356		7.50	1875	169	1.50	2778	250	1110

Source: Mironov (1992) in Moon (2001), p. 12.
Note: Obligations are means for male serfs. Direct taxes comprise a household tax to 1723 and a poll tax from 1724. Index A reports nominal values. Index B is deflated by the grain-price series. Labor services (barshchina) are calculated using area of land cultivated and value of cultivated output.

production, since they could allocate time between cultivation and other activities, unlike the *barshchina* serfs. For example, it has been estimated that by the mid-nineteenth century, estate owners were responsible for 90 percent of grain supplied to domestic and export markets, and serfs were responsible for 10 percent (Blum 1961, 390–392).

Serfs were to perform all tasks, within reason, requested by the estate owner. Many of these duties related to agriculture but they were not limited to this sector. Historically, members of the small merchant class established and participated in large-scale manufacturing, but nobles and peasants began to establish manufacturing firms beginning in the 1760s. By 1813–14, nobles accounted for 64 percent of mining firms, 78 percent of woolen-cloth firms, 60 percent of paper mills, 66 percent of crystal and glass works, and 80 percent of potash works. As partial fulfillment of serfs' *barshchina* obligation, serfowners could require serfs to work in these firms. It is believed that the number of serfs owning small factories was large, but relatively few owned large enterprises or became million-aires.[8] One of the most striking features of the peasant industrialist was not his or her ability to establish and operate a factory or other business. Of greater interest is the fact that these serfs employed free persons, often to perform menial tasks, and sometimes owned serfs themselves.[9]

The End-of-Serfdom Debate

There was a reinvigorated debate concerning the factors influencing the adoption of slavery and serfdom and factors affecting the end of serfdom in Russia and the end of slavery elsewhere among economic historians in the 1970s and early 1980s. The topics were worthy of debate, because there have been many equilibrium paths to the adoption and elimination of in-stitutionalized forced labor across time and space. Among the theories put forward concerning the abolition of serfdom were political and military *raisons d'état*, cultural factors, fear of serf revolt, the general "crisis of serfdom," and the unprofitability of serfdom.

Blum (1961) points to several hypotheses, including the spread of hu-manitarian and liberal ideas among Russian intellectuals and nobility, fear of serf revolt, Russian defeat in the Crimean War, and political *raisons d'état*. It is the last explanation he finds most credible, or at least the least suspect. Tsar Alexander II was convinced that Russia had begun

---

[8] Blum (1961, 297–298). Landowners engaged in manufacturing remained a minority, however, and most continued in agricultural production.

[9] See Blum (1961, 298–301) for a discussion of the Nikita Demidov (a serf) and Shereme-tev serfs' examples.

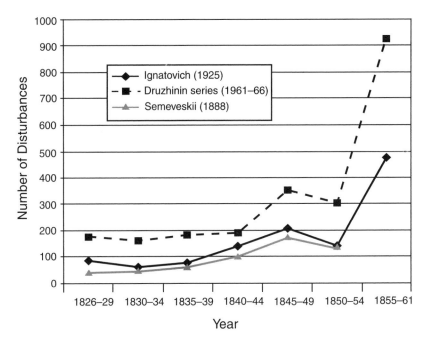

Figure 8.1 "Peasant disturbances," Russia, 1826–61. (Source: Moon 2001.)

Pokrovskii (1924) deserves special attention, because the research spawned a particularly lively debate among economic historians in the mid-1980s. He argues, but does not convincingly demonstrate, that serfdom became unprofitable and led to the abolition of serfdom. Historians and political scientists have brought considerable evidence to bear to the contrary. Domar and Machina (1984) subject this hypothesis to econometric tests, and they cannot reject the hypothesis that serfdom was still profitable. Toumanoff (1973) revises and extends their theoretical analysis and concludes that voluntary manumission would have been the appropriate empirical evidence to use to demonstrate that serfdom was unprofitable.

While researchers have been able to reject hypotheses, such as the unprofitability of serfdom, the debate is still open with respect to the set of likely determinants, or, more precisely, the weight assigned various likely determinants. This debate will not be settled in this paper, but the paper's modest goal is to review each major theory. In the following sections, I survey the principal emancipation schemes considered and implementation of the 1861 Emancipation Statutes, compare the Russian and other emancipation schemes, and offer suggestions for contemporary Sudan.

conversion of peasants dues, or *obrok*, under "temporary obligation" and of payments in arrears into labor on the landowners' estate; labor demanded from peasants in exchange for access to meadows, pastures, water sources, and land severed from their previous allotments; and lending by landowners in which peasants were obliged to work off interest. As in the American South, the institution of sharecropping also emerged. In Russia, peasants were often rented land by the estate owners and required to make payments in terms of output, typically half, from the land.[14] Further and in contrast to the emancipation of slaves in the American South, dependence on estate owners was effectively extended by the continued prohibition on movement by serfs. The upshot of such policies, practices, and institutions is that, rather than being simple and abrupt, the process of manumission was complex and slow.

The redemption program was designed to create a broad class of landowning peasants, known as "peasant-proprietors," who would be independent of the noble landowners. The terms of the redemption program were favorable to the estate owners in order to provide an incentive to opt into the program. In addition to compensating landowners, the program was initially voluntary for the landowner but obligatory for the former serf once the landowner decided to engage in the redemption process.

The program proceeded as follows. The peasant and estate owner agreed on a land allotment for purchase by the peasant, a minimum for which was set in the Statutes. Most allotments permitted to be redeemed were lands in permanent use during temporary obligation. The redemption amount did not depend on the market price of land. Instead, it was calculated using the cash dues peasants paid to estate owners for the use of their allotments during temporary obligation. Few serfs could finance the entire redemption payment. Therefore, the Russian government advanced the estate owner 75 to 80 percent of the redemption amount in bank notes and long-term bonds earning annual interest of five percent. Freed serfs would be responsible for paying estate owners the remaining 20 to 25 percent of the redemption amount.[15] The peasants' government-financed mortgage was fixed at a rate of six percent annual interest and for a term of 49 years. Peasants could not contract individually to redeem their allotments. Rather, peasants were obliged to contract jointly with

---

[14] In fact, this system was identical to the institution of *obrok* payment in kind under serfdom. See Moon (2001) for a fuller discussion of post-abolition practices by which serfdom was effectively extended.

[15] The redemption amount was calculated using the stream of income from cash dues peasants owed estate owners following "temporary obligation." Peasants were to pay all the redemption-related payments to the government rather than directly to estate owners. However, peasants were often required to "work off" redemption payments owed the estate owners as in the cases mentioned above.

TABLE 8.6
Redemption Payments and Prices for Land, Loitsky Series

Region	Land Allotment (000s des.)	Value of land at market prices (R, millions)		Value of land, redemption value (R, millions)	Redemption value, % market prices 1863–72
		1854–58	1863–72		
Russia and Left-Bank Ukraine					
Non-black earth	12186	155	180	342	190.0
Black earth	9841	219	284	342	120.0
Western provinces	10141	170	184	183	100.0
Total	32168	544	648	867	136.7

Source: Gershchenkron (1965).
Note: Entry for Total in final column is mean redemption value to market price.

In general, architects of emancipation schemes have assigned more, if not all, weight to the property rights of the owners of serfs or slaves rather than to those of the serfs or slaves. Like most schemes of gradual emancipation over time and around the world, the Russian abolition program required that the direct financial cost of freedom for serfs be borne by the unfree persons themselves. Further, as Engerman (1996) finds in his survey of emancipations in the Americas, Europe, Africa, and Asia, compensation was not paid to serfs and slaves in these emancipation programs. Goldin (1973) also shows complete expropriation of slaveowner property to be missing in emancipation programs in the Western Hemisphere. In striking contrast to the case of the northeastern United States in the late 1700s and early 1800s, the debate among serfowners was neither whether they would be compensated nor who should pay compensation, but rather the magnitude of compensation in Russia that was contentious.[17]

Another characteristic of emancipation programs is their historical clustering. Engerman (1996) shows that most emancipations around the world happened between the late eighteenth and late nineteenth centuries. There was also clustering in subperiods: 11 between 1801 and 1820, five between 1831 and 1832, 13 between 1841 and 1850, and 4 between 1851 and 1864. By extension, international pressure in favor of abolition increased over the period such that late emancipators became more isolated over time.

[17] Freed serfs' freedom of movement was also a bone of contention. See Engerman and Fogel (1974) for a rich analysis of gradual emancipation in the United States and Great Britain.

with slavery and government indifference to or complicity in the practice, temporary guardianship by individual slaveowners or the state, or gradual emancipation more generally, may not be credible. It may encourage, for example, more intensive use of slaves or trafficking of slaves to areas where forced labor also remains.[20] *Ceteris paribus*, it appears that the more credible policy option is immediate emancipation.

Evidence from Russia and the United States suggests that at least one desirable and two undesirable outcomes resulted, regardless of intended speed of reform. The common desirable outcome was that former serfs and slaves were ultimately able to acquire land in significant numbers. In Russia, the amount of land peasants owned rose from 6.5 to 23.5 million *desiatinii* between 1877 and 1907; and in the United States by the 1890s, nearly 25 percent of southern black farmers owned their land (Moon 2001, 112). With respect to less desirable outcomes, former serfs in Russia were not permitted to leave their land, and, beginning in the 1890s in the United States, blacks faced restrictions on movement, among other things, as segregationist laws and practices were adopted in the South and then nationwide.

A second undesirable outcome was the emergence of the sharecropping system in the place of serfdom and slavery. Would one institution replace another in Sudan? This is difficult to know. We would need data on labor-market conditions and former slaves' opportunities. As a poor, developing country, on the border between medium and low development in the UN Human Development Index with a GDP per capita of $1890, it likely has a relatively high unemployment rate and a high proportion of unskilled workers in the labor market.[21] It would be reasonable to infer that the marginal rate of substitution between free and non-free unskilled labor would be high.[22] But this assumes a flexible, freely adjusting labor market with profit-maximizing owners.[23] This assumption may be too strong, given the limited data we have on owner preferences and behavior and the motives for and implementation of continued slavery in Sudan.

[20] Engerman and Fogel (1974) and Goldin (1973) identify the intensification of work by slaves, slave smuggling, and other drawbacks of implementing gradual emancipation around the world and over time.

[21] Sudan ranks at the bottom of the "medium development" UN classification, but this ranking is based on data from northern Sudan, which is historically better off than southern Sudan. See UNDP (2004).

[22] A high marginal rate of substitution assumes that tasks being performed by forced labor are suitable for unskilled labor. Certainly, this issue is complicated by war. As a result of slaves' abductions from contested areas, is their proper designation "slaves" or "prisoners of war," or something else?

[23] See Karlan and Krueger, (Chapter 1) and Rogers and Swinnerton (Chapter 2) in this volume for elaboration of labor-market supply and demand conditions.

Gershchenkron, Alexander (1962), *Economic Backwardness in Historical Perspective*. Cambridge, MA: Harvard University Press.

Gershchenkron, Alexander (1965), "Agrarian Policies and Industrialization: Russia, 1861–1917," in M. M. Postan and H. J. Habakkuk (eds), *Cambridge Economic History of Europe*, vol. 6, part 2, (Cambridge: Cambridge University Press).

Goldin, Claudia (1973), "The Economics of Emancipation," *Journal of Economic History* 33(1): 66–85.

Gregory, Paul (1994), *Before Command: An Economic History of Russia from Emancipation to the First Five-Year Plan*. Princeton: Princeton University Press.

Hoch, S. L., and W. R. Augustine (2001), "The Tax Censuses and the Decline of the Serf Population in Imperial Russia, 1833–1858," in David Moon, *The Abolition of Serfdom in Russia* (Harlow: Longman).

Kahan, Arcadius (1973), "Notes on Serfdom in Western and Eastern Europe," *Journal of Economic History* 33(1): 86–99.

Koval'chenko, I. D. (1967), *Russkoe krepostnoe krest'ianstvo v pervoi polovine XIX v. (The Russian Serf Peasantry in the First Half of the 19th Century)*. Moscow: Izdatel'stvo Moskovskogo Universiteta.

Lyashchenko, P. I. (1949), *History of the National Economy of Russia to the 1917 Revolution*, trans. L. H. Herman. New York: Macmillan.

Moon, David (2001), *The Abolition of Serfdom in Russia*. Harlow, England: Longman.

Nazer, Mende, and Damien Lewis (2004), *Slave*. London: Public Affairs.

Nechkina, M. V. (1962), *Revoliutsionnaia situatsiia v Rossii v 1859–1861 gg. (The Revolutionary Situation in Russia in 1859–1861)*, trans. Terence Emmons. Moscow: Izdatel'stvo Akademii Nauk SSSR.

Pokrovskii, M. N. (1924), *Russkaia istoriia s drevneishikh veremen. Tom 4. Izdanie piatoe (Russian History from Earliest Times*, vol. 4, 5th ed.), trans. Erica Brendel. Leningrad: Gosudarstvennoe izdaltel'stvo.

Rieber, Alfred J. ed. (1966), T*he Politics of Autocracy: Letters of Alexander II to Prince A. I. Bariatinskii*. Paris: Mouton and Company.

Rift Valley Institute (2003), "Sudan Abduction and Slavery Project: Abductee Database Report 2003," *www.riftvalley.net/inside/projects.htm*.

Toumanoff, Peter G. (1973), "The Profitability of Serfdom: A Comment," *Journal of Economic History* 45(4): 955–959.

Troinitskii, A. (1861), *The Serf Population in Russia According to the Tenth National Census*, trans. Elaine Herman. St. Petersburg: Karl Vul'f Press.

United Nations Development Programme (UNDP). (2004). *Human Development Report 2004, hdr.undp.org/reports/global/2004/*.

U.S. State Department, Bureau of African Affairs (2002), *Slavery, Abduction and Forced Servitude in Sudan, Report of the International Eminent Persons Group (2002), www.state.gov/documents/organization/11951.pdf*.

Vasagar, Jeevan (2004), "Where Straight Hair Is One of Slavery's Legacies," *Manchester Guardian Weekly*, 23–29 July.

By the time of the American Revolution, difficulty in reconciling slavery with ideals of liberty and equality that Americans espoused began to call into question the institution of slavery, and with it, the validity of a master's claim to compensation for the loss of those individuals he purported to own. At the same time, however, public discussion on how slavery might be ended repeatedly raised the possibility of compensation to masters. Those who regretted the persistence of slavery and viewed it as an unfortunate legacy of the colonial period suggested that freeing slaves by compensating their masters was a way of solving the problem and doing justice to all concerned. Debates on the Constitution underscored the enormous investment that slavery represented to Southerners, thus early proposals often contained suggestions that African Americans might be emancipated by using the proceeds of the sale of western lands to compensate slaveowners. Recognizing the property right of slaveholders and offering compensation attempted to indemnify them for the losses that emancipation would entail. Supporters of these proposals hoped that compensation would win them the support of at least some slaveowners. Their hopes were disappointed and these early proposals came to nothing as the South rejected the idea out of hand, and white Americans more generally were unwilling to forego the revenue that accrued from the sale of public lands (see Fladeland 1976).

In the late eighteenth century, religious concerns about slavery built on the political doubts which arose during the Revolutionary era (see Loveland 1966). This questioning of slavery was often paired with the possibility of compensation for slaveowners in what was understood as a need to do justice to masters and slaves alike. Manumission societies formed in the border states to undertake slave redemption as part of a program to end slavery. Quakers in particular sought to balance the interest of the slave and that of his or her master. Thus they bought and freed slaves in order to live up to their long-standing testimony against slavery. By 1830, for example, North Carolina Quakers had spent nearly $13,000 to ransom slaves. By these means, more than 600 slaves were freed in that state. However, a significant number of the slaves thus freed were elderly or invalids unable to care for themselves, and the Quakers found they had to become guardians to them. More importantly, as racial and economic rationales for the persistence of slavery strengthened in the nineteenth century, southern Quakers became a dissident minority in an environment in which slavery became increasingly difficult to question. Ultimately the efforts of these societies freed very few slaves and did little to undermine slavery as an institution (see Weeks 1896, 224–229).

In 1817, the American Colonization Society was founded with a view to ending slavery gradually. By compensating slaveholders who emancipated their slaves and transporting free blacks to Liberia, colonizationists

would be to participate in the sin. "[I]t is wrong," he wrote in an editorial in *The Liberator* in June of 1832, "and consequently sinful, to give money, or any other pretended equivalent, for 'the bodies and souls of men,' under any pretence whatever." Garrison's comment suggests that among the many aspects of compensation that troubled him was the perception that when an abolitionist purchased an enslaved person's freedom, that abolitionist became, however briefly, a slaveowner. A month later, Garrison reiterated, "[it] is the duty of the owners of slaves to liberate their victims immediately—they deserve and should receive no remuneration for giving up stolen property" (*Liberator*, 14 July 1832). In vitriolic editorials, pamphlets, and speeches, Garrisonian abolitionists denounced compensation and began to call for immediate abolition.

When Garrison and his followers met to form the American Antislavery Society (AASS) the following year in Philadelphia, they drafted a Declaration of Sentiments that included the following proclamation (*Liberator*, 21 August 1857):

> We maintain, that no compensation should be given to planters emancipating their slaves, because it would be a surrender of the great fundamental principle, that man cannot hold property in man; because slavery is a crime, and therefore [the slave] is not an article to be sold; because the holders of slaves are not the just proprietors of what they claim—freeing the slaves is not depriving them of property, but restoring it to the right owner—it is not wronging the master, but righting the slave, restoring him to himself.

The resolve of the new association could scarcely have been more unequivocal.

Despite this strengthening conviction, American abolitionists had to reconsider the issue of compensation immediately. In the same year that the American Antislavery Society was founded, the British government legislated the abolition of slavery in its possessions by enacting a program of compensated emancipation. In the British West Indies, slaves were to serve an apprenticeship of five years and then be freed. West Indian planters would receive twenty million pounds in compensation from the British government. Eager to differentiate themselves from their erstwhile colonial masters, American abolitionists criticized compensation ever more fiercely. Garrison, traveling in England at the time the bill was before Parliament, reported to the *Liberator* in September 1833 that compensation was "justly viewed as money bestowed where no loss can be proved, . . . an abandonment of the high ground of justice." Comments such as this suggest that American abolitionists envisioned a better, purer form of emancipation in which slaveholders would repent and would require no inducements to let their slaves go free.

a more tenacious grasp," Douglass wrote in 1849 (*The North Star*, 13 July):

> I would simply advise every man, woman and child, whether black, white, or yellow, that so long as they are guiltless of crime, they have a right to freedom. It is theirs. The idea of making them pay for what is their own by the inalienable gift of their Creator, is most absurd, preposterous, and Heaven insulting.

Similarly, although in slavery he had worked hard to raise enough money to free himself, once he had escaped from bondage, William Wells Brown scorned a former master's offer to sell his freedom to Boston abolitionists. "I cannot accept of Mr. Price's offer to become a purchaser of my body and soul," he insisted. "God made me as free as he did Enoch Price, and Mr. Price shall never receive a dollar from me or my friends with my consent" (Brown 1849, ix). Henry Bibb, a former fugitive, argued in his Canadian newspaper that the practice of paying for escaped slaves was counterproductive. "A great mistake has been made here in the north, by purchasing the freedom of fugitive slaves . . . it has only served to stimulate the hunt for fugitives." Bibb went on to suggest that rather than ransoming fugitive slaves, they should be permitted to be returned to the South, where they could instruct their peers about life in the free states and thus disrupt the system from within (*Voice of the Fugitive*, 5 November 1851). Defiantly, black abolitionists rejected the idea that their bodies were commodities to be bought and sold.

The great paradox, however, was that although white and black antislavery activists were for the most part unanimous in their opposition to compensation or to buying the freedom of fugitive slaves, almost everyone in the abolitionist community was involved in redeeming slaves in one way or another. Black churches routinely canvassed their members to ransom the relatives of members of their congregations (see Finkenbine 1993, 180–181). Former slaves published narratives of their lives expressly to raise money to ransom family members. White and black antislavery newspapers carried notices attesting to the honesty of various African Americans attempting to raise money to free themselves or their family members. White abolitionists who belonged to antislavery organizations that explicitly denounced compensation contributed money to help buy individual blacks out of slavery. Henry Ward Beecher staged slave "auctions" in his Brooklyn church to raise money to purchase freedom for a number of young slave women. Even Garrison himself contributed to the "ransom" of Douglass, arguing that the particular circumstances of the case were such that compassion and prudence had to take precedence over principle. "To save a fellow-being," he wrote in the *Liberator* in

ical issues were not raised, slave redemption was rarely a straightforward proposition.

As almost every free black family had relatives still in bondage, thousands of African American families went through experiences such as these. Kelley was fortunate in that he was literate and had friends and acquaintances to help him in his efforts to be reunited with his family. Other fugitives, without friends or money, found it almost impossible to maintain ties with family members in the South. For fugitives, especially following the Fugitive Slave Act of 1850, communicating with a former master in hopes of arranging the purchase of a spouse or child meant revealing their location and thus running the risk of recapture. Returning to the South to fetch family members involved still more dangers. Even if legally emancipated, freed people had few levers with which to pressure former masters to relinquish their kin. The occupational opportunities open to African Americans meant that the accumulation of the necessary funds required enormous efforts. When the money had finally been saved, legal problems and the difficulties of transporting money over long distances remained to be overcome. Since a slave could not purchase another slave, agents had to be employed, and these were not always trustworthy. There were few guarantees that the master would live up to his promise and little recourse if he failed to do so. Yet painstakingly, despite all these obstacles, black families struggled to redeem their loved ones.

For those still enslaved and hoping to purchase their liberty, the desire for freedom forced hard choices at almost every turn. Typically, one family member managed to free him or herself and then worked to purchase those still enslaved. Yet self-purchase was particularly fraught with difficulties, as whatever a slave earned or owned legally belonged to his or her master. Arrangements could be struck, but a master might renege, as Moses Grandy learned to his sorrow. Grandy paid his purchase price three times over before finally achieving his freedom (Grandy 1843). Lunsford Lane worked diligently for years to free himself and his family, but he found that local white communities could take offense if a slave was seen to be too successful (Lane 1842). In addition, laws requiring manumitted blacks to leave southern states meant that the pursuit of freedom often entailed years of separation. Even the decision about who should seek freedom first was fraught with difficulties. Arguably it made more sense for a man to purchase his freedom first because he could earn more money and then free the rest of his family more rapidly. Against that, if a black woman remained behind in slavery, any children she might have would be born slaves and thus would also have to be ransomed, raising the amount of money needed considerably. In addition, if an enslaved woman's husband left the neighborhood, she might be forced into another relationship. Either way, the desire for freedom could lead to

contradicted Southern assertions that family ties mattered little to their slaves. Similarly, racist attitudes regarding the sexual mores of African Americans could be rebutted by references to black men and women who labored long and hard to free their spouses and demonstrated fidelity that lasted over years of separation. The slave who freed himself and his family by virtue of his own efforts also contradicted the images of indolence and dependency that attached to freed people in the minds of many northerners. The image of black men toiling resolutely for their own freedom offered a nonthreatening image of black manhood that allayed white fears of racial violence. It also accorded well with the ideal of the self-made man, an ideal espoused by many white abolitionists. Though they may have deplored the notion of compensation in principle, the logic of the antislavery argument itself compelled white antislavery activists to encourage and to contribute to the efforts of the enslaved to emancipate themselves in this way. In turn, such former slaves became powerful advertisements for abolitionist arguments about African-American character and the essential justice of emancipation.

White abolitionists were even more willing to contribute money to redeem a slave when the slave in question was female, and especially if the woman was young and light-skinned. In their campaign to build public support for abolition, antislavery writers frequently linked slaveowning with the sexual exploitation of enslaved women. Lurid comparisons between southern plantations and "oriental" harems constituted a powerful tool to mobilize antislavery public opinion. Eager to extract the maximum impact from these images (and for the most part oblivious to the racist implications of the strategy), antislavery writers emphasized that light-skinned or mulatto women were most at risk of sexual exploitation and therefore most in need of rescue. Fictional accounts such as Lydia Maria Child's short story "The Quadroons" (1842) or slave narratives such as that of Louisa Picquet described the vulnerability and abuse of such women in terms that appealed directly to nineteenth-century ideals of feminine purity. As such they mandated a response. Picquet's narrative was published in 1861 with the explicit intention of generating funds to redeem her mother. It begins with a description of Picquet as "a little above the medium height, easy and graceful in her manners, of fair complexion and rosy cheeks, with dark eyes, a flowing head of hair with no perceptible inclination to curl, and every appearance, at first view, of an accomplished white lady," and continues with attestations of her church membership and exemplary character. However, the substance of the narrative consists of Picquet's efforts to resist the advances of various owners. The account concludes with appeals to assist her in her efforts to ransom her mother (Picquet and Mattison 1861). Picquet's narrative invoked the twin values of filial piety and female purity, thus questions of the probity of slave

Responses to the question of the redemption of enslaved African Americans varied over time and according to the political situation, but also according to whose rescue was being proposed. The aftermath of independence set some Americans to thinking about the conflict between slavery and the values of the American Revolution, and searching for ways in which the interests of slaveowners and the enslaved might be reconciled and slavery ended. In that context, solutions that involved compensation to slaveholders who manumitted their slaves seemed reasonable. However, once the demand for immediate abolition emerged, many antislavery activists rejected compensation. As the founding documents of the AASS and the furor over Douglass's purchase make clear, by the 1830s and 1840s the formal position of most American abolitionists on the question of compensation to slaveholders had become fairly categorical. Slaveholding was denounced as a crime, and antislavery activists rejected any suggestion that the "criminals" should receive any compensation. Using the language of evangelical righteousness, abolitionists argued publicly and vociferously that it was inappropriate to bribe a sinner to cease his transgressions.

Yet as the debate over Douglass's ransom demonstrated, loud though their protests might be, abolitionists were neither unanimous nor entirely consistent in their objections to slave redemption. Throughout the period black families went to heroic lengths to raise the money to rescue their loved ones from bondage. Moreover, whether they condoned or denounced compensation, black and white antislavery activists actively involved themselves in the redemption of enslaved African Americans. Although they knew very well that there were good reasons not to do it, when the slave in question was someone known, or when the slave's situation resonated with prevailing cultural norms, abolitionists, black and white, set their principles to one side and ransomed thousands of slaves out of bondage. As Lindley Coates acknowledged when he criticized Garrison's support for the ransom of Frederick Douglass (*Liberator*, 12 July 1834):

> When a self-emancipated man has come soliciting money to ransom his wife and children still in bondage, we have had a hard struggle of doubt, whether it was right to give him assistance or not, but a feeling of humanity for the individual victims to be ransomed has overcome the sense of the wrong thereby done to the mass of the enslaved.

When brought face to face with the real suffering engendered by slavery, few abolitionists found they could place righteousness before compassion. As in so many instances, ideological purity and humanity coexisted at best uneasily. Confronted with this dilemma, most abolitionists appear to have opted for humanity.

Chapter Ten

Frederick Douglass and the Politics of Slave Redemptions

JOHN STAUFFER

Throughout his career as an abolitionist, Frederick Douglass's most passionate desire was an immediate end to slavery. He was, like most other "immediatists," a millennialist: freedom represented a new age and a sharp break from the sins of the past and linear chronology. Emancipation filled Douglass with extraordinary hope and possibility, and he worshipped it with unwavering faith. In fact his swift rise to fame, and his extraordinary productivity during his twenty-year tenure as an abolitionist, depended on his faith that emancipation, and thus a new world, was at hand.

But Douglass was also comparatively pragmatic about exactly how emancipation would be achieved. As a member of William Lloyd Garrison's American Anti-Slavery Society from 1841 to 1849, he espoused Garrison's policy of nonresistance, which viewed government as corrupt and relied on nonviolence and moral suasion to end slavery. He sometimes argued, following the Society's policy, that compensating slaveholders to emancipate their slaves amounted to complicity in the sin of slavery. Yet even as a Garrisonian nonresister, Douglass often championed instances of emancipation that involved payment to owners or acts of violence. In 1846 British sympathizers purchased his legal freedom from his master, for which he was grateful. He valorized in speeches and fiction the achievement of Madison Washington, who imitated "*George Washington*" in gaining liberty through controlled and heroic violence (Douglass 1979–92 [hereafter TFDP] 1:1 [1845], 68). And he continually pointed to his famous fight with Edward Covey as the turning point in his life as slave; it was through this act of violence that he became free "in *fact*," if still a slave "in *form*" (Douglass [1855] 2003, [hereafter *My Bondage*], 140).

After Douglass moved to Rochester, New York, a hotbed of political abolitionism, and became an independent newspaperman, his views of government and the means to emancipation began to change. He accepted the Constitution as an antislavery document, transformed his newspaper into a political abolitionist newspaper, and embraced violence

America were he to remain a fugitive. "I think the very best thing was done in letting Master Hugh have the hundred and fifty pounds sterling and leaving me free to return to my appropriate field of labor," he concluded (225).

Douglass acknowledged an uneasiness with the transaction, but it related to its nature, rather than to the principle of compensation. It was ransom money, paid to allay the risk of recapture, not as payment for his person, as he noted. But in one sense, the sum did relate to his person: "Had I been a private person, having no other relations or duties than those of a personal and family nature, I should never have consented to the payment of so large a sum" (225–226). A smaller sum paid for a "private person" was evidently an acceptable form of compensation as well. In his farewell speech to the British people, on 30 March 1847, he said that he would never have solicited friends to purchase his freedom or raise money for his freedom. That would have been improper. But given that it was done "from the prompting or suggestion of their [his friends'] own hearts, entirely independent of myself," he was deeply grateful (TFDP 1:2 [1847], 43). As a result, he did not have to shoulder "the responsibility of the act," and so believed that "no right or noble principle" was "sacrificed in the transaction" (TFDP 1:2 [1847], 43–44). Having someone else pay ransom money to purchase your freedom was ethically acceptable; doing it yourself was not.

Douglass had a similar problem when ex-slaves purchased their own freedom or those of family members. In 1849 he reprinted in his newspaper the story of an ex-slave, John Douglass, who raised money to purchase the freedom of his mother (for $200 down plus $100 in future payments). In an editorial Douglass chided the man for his actions: "I do not, in any shape or manner, approve or wish to have anything to do with the purchase of slaves," he wrote, apparently ignoring his own purchase (Douglass 1849). But then he qualified his denunciation of slave purchases: "I cannot allow the right of any human being to claim payment for permitting any other human being to go where he or she desires to go. It is a natural right of every man and woman in God's universe" (Douglass 1849). It came down to a matter of power; a slave (or ex-slave) was powerless in negotiating for his or his family's freedom. But friends seeking to change the legal status of a fugitive, who was already free in form, could negotiate from a position of strength. Douglass emphasized the unnatural power imbalance between master and slave, and the natural, God-given equity between people, by stating: "This woman had just as much right" to ask her slave master "for payment that he might be allowed to go where he would, as he had to make this demand upon her." "Besides," he added, "every act of purchase enhances the market value of human chattels; and makes the monsters cling to their *property* with a

By the late 1840s, Douglass began to interpret the Constitution not as a proslavery document, as Garrisonians and slaveowners did, but as a sacred antislavery text. He changed the name of his newspaper to *Frederick Douglass' Paper* to reflect his newfound faith in political action; Smith helped fund it and suggested its name.

Gerrit Smith was one of the wealthiest men in the country, and gave most of his money to the poor and downtrodden. He purchased the liberty of scores of slaves, paid their way to free states, and helped them resettle (often in his village of Peterboro, New York) and find employment. Through such acts he transformed his farm community of Madison County, New York, into a model interracial community. And in 1846 he undertook one of the largest philanthropic acts in the nineteenth century: he gave away 120,000 acres to some 3000 poor, landless New York State blacks, amounting to forty acres a person, which represented a rehearsal for Reconstruction and anticipated the plea among freedmen and women for "40 acres and a mule" to start a new life (Stauffer 2002, 144). Smith's land was in the Adirondacks, in Franklin and Essex counties, and partly because neither Smith nor the recipients of his gift had the cash to buy mules and supplies to start life anew as independent farmers, only about eighty families settled at "Timbucto," as they called their settlement (Stauffer 2002, 141). But John Brown settled there with his family; it was there where he conceived his scheme to invade the South; and he considered Timbucto his permanent home from 1848 until his death at Harpers Ferry. Douglass lauded Smith's gift and urged recipients to save their money for the move. For both men, Timbucto was a model interracial community and a form of compensated emancipation—for oppressed and poor blacks, rather than racist oppressors.

In 1855, Smith and Douglass applied this vision of compensation for the oppressed to a new political party they helped found: the Radical Abolition party, which advocated the redistribution of land so that "no man" would be "rich" and "no man" "poor," as Smith put it (Stauffer 2002, 137). They viewed such redistribution of land as part of their larger efforts to end all evil; in fact the platform of the Radical Abolition party advocated an immediate end to slavery, through negotiation if possible, force if necessary, as well as land for all ex-slaves. Throughout the 1850s, Douglass and Smith understood the need to negotiate with the South from a position of force—whether through monetary enticements to end slavery, or violent intervention.

Smith's numerous purchases of slaves and his gifts of land to poor blacks led to more formal proposals for compensated emancipation. With Douglass stumping for him, he was elected to Congress in 1852, and in his April 1854 speech on the Kansas-Nebraska bill, which repealed the Missouri Compromise and opened northern territories to slavery, he

and urged him to reply to William Lloyd Garrison's derisive attack of Smith's proposal. "Do write a reply to [Garrison's] most unfair treatment of your speech, and send it to the *Liberator*," Douglass urged his friend (Douglass 1857, October 13).

Douglass's greatest support for the idea of compensated emancipation was expressed in his speeches commemorating British West Indian emancipation. American blacks began celebrating West Indian emancipation on August 1, 1834, the day legal slavery ended in the British West Indies; and soon August 1 became a sacred day that rivaled the Fourth of July (TFDP 1:3 [1858], 227). By the 1840s, August 1 celebrations had become integrated affairs, though typically with more blacks than whites in attendance (Jeffrey 2006). From 1847 until his death in 1895 Douglass gave over twenty speeches celebrating West Indian emancipation. For most of his life he viewed the event as the "greatest and grandest of the nineteenth century," as he put it in 1847 (TFDP 1:2 [1847], 69). Ten years later he said much the same thing: West Indian emancipation was "of vast and sublime significance, surpassing all power of exaggeration" (TFDP 1:3 [1857], 191). It was "the most interesting and sublime event of the nineteenth century" (194):

> It was the triumph of a great moral principle, a decisive victory, after a severe and protracted struggle, of freedom over slavery; of justice and mercy against a grim and bloody system of devilish brutality. It was an acknowledgement by a great nation of the sacredness of humanity, as against the claims of power and cupidity.

He saw in British emancipation a typology or foreshadowing of the American millennium, a kind of Second Coming on a national scale. "There was something Godlike in this decree of the British nation. It was the spirit of the Son of God commanding the devil of slavery to go out of the British West Indies" (TFDP 1:3 [1857], 190).

Nowhere was Douglass so optimistic about the new age than in his August 1 speeches, which are among his best: "We live in stirring times, and amid thrilling events," he said in his celebration speech of 1848, the same year that France abolished slavery in the French West Indies (TFDP 1:2 [1848], 135):

> There is no telling what a day may bring forth. The human mind is everywhere filled with expectation. The moral sky is studded with signs and wonder. . . . Liberty rides as on a chariot of fire. . . . The grand conflict of the angel Liberty with the monster Slavery has at last come. The globe shakes with the contest. I thank God that I am permitted, with you, to live in these days, and to participate humbly, in this struggle.

or failure of slavery, as a money-making system, determines with many whether the thing is virtuous or villainous, and whether it should be maintained or abolished" (TFDP 1:3 [1857], 198).

Douglass knew as early as the late 1840s that some form of compensation would be needed before slavery could end in America. It would take the form either of ransom money, or of blood money, as he later said. In England, emancipation was bought "with money," in America, "with blood" (TFDP 1:5 [1885], 196). War was politics by other means, which required different forms of compensation. But Douglass believed that in both events, the main impetus for emancipation came not from offers of compensation, but from God, with abolitionists bearing witness to God's truth. As Douglass put it: "had slavery been abolished simply by the sword, it would have revived as soon as the sword was returned to its scappard" (TFDP 1:5 [1885], 199). What he never acknowledged was that a peaceful, compensated emancipation would have been far preferable to the apocalypse of war that brought immediate emancipation, even though southern states consistently rejected such proposals. After losing the war to end slavery, white southerners redeemed themselves by retaliating against blacks and preserving the old hierarchy. The century of horrible racism and racial oppression following the war stemmed in part from the violence that brought slavery to an end. Far more than their counterparts in the British West Indies, American freedmen and women lived in a state of "war" and were continually subjected to "terror, intimidation, and violence" (Litwack 1998, xi, xiii). Slavery was revived, though in extralegal forms, "as soon as the sword was returned to its scappard."

Bibliography

Douglass, Frederick ([1845] 2003), *Narrative of the Life of Frederick Douglass, An American Slave, Written by Himself*, edited by David W. Blight. Boston: Bedford/ St. Martins.

Douglass, Frederick (1849), "Buying a Mother's Freedom," *North Star*, July 13.

Douglass, Frederick ([1855] 2003), *My Bondage and My Freedom*, edited by John Stauffer. New York: The Modern Library.

Douglass, Frederick (1857), Letters, Frederick Douglass to Gerrit Smith, 18 August and 13 October 1857. The Gerrit Smith Papers, Syracuse University (and on microfilm).

Douglass, Frederick (1950), *The Life and Writings of Frederick Douglass*, vols. 1–5, edited by Philip S. Foner. New York: International Publishers.

Douglass, Frederick (1979–92), *The Frederick Douglass Papers* (TFDP), series 1, vols. 1–5, edited by John Blassingame. New Haven: Yale University Press.

Fladeland, Betty L. (1976), "Compensated Emancipation: A Rejected Alternative," *Journal of Southern History*, 42(2): 169–186.

Part IV

PHILOSOPHICAL CONSIDERATIONS

Chapter Eleven

The Moral Quandary of Slave Redemption

HOWARD McGARY

Slave redemption programs invoke feelings of discomfort in some people. And this discomfort sometimes continues to exist even in people who ultimately endorse such efforts. Some of these people are troubled because they question whether the good outweighs the bad. A number of papers in this volume address this concern. However, the source of this discomfort can also be attributed to the belief that it is wrong to always order the overall value of the states of affairs produced by alternative actions, and on the basis of these results, make a determination about what we ought to do. These critics, who have been labeled ethical deontologists, believe that it is morally wrong, at least in some instances, to bring about the best overall states of affairs based on prior rankings of value. According to the deontologist, there are certain duties and correlated rights that are absolute and should not be violated even if doing so produces the most overall good. The philosopher Immanuel Kant is most often associated with this way of thinking.

The strict deontological way of looking at things draws a sharp distinction between the right and the good, and gives priority to the right over the good. Consequentialists or teleologists, on the other hand, derive their conceptions of right from the good. For them, the right thing to do is determined by promoting or maximizing overall good. For the deontologist, it is our motives for acting rather than the outcomes of our actions that should determine our duties. Doing things for the right reason is crucial for the deontologist.

In the debate over slave redemption programs, the critics of such efforts don't deny that in some cases the good is achieved by purchasing slaves. Nonetheless, these critics believe that by purchasing slaves the redeemers are giving incorrect priority to the good over the right. For them there are some things that should not be done, and by failing to stand against these things, we cannot be correctly described as moral persons. Is this a viable conclusion? I have given two reasons why some people object to slave redemption efforts. The first reason focuses on the doubts that some people have about whether such efforts will actually do more harm than good. The second reason relies on the idea that the buying and

To free slaves by purchasing them is to participate in the commodifying of human beings, which deontological principles plausibly prohibit. But that would be to embrace an extraordinarily strong prohibition that might rule out cases in which we believe that it can be morally appropriate and even required to calculate how much a person's life or limbs are worth because of an accident or negligence.

The model of slavery that is often referred to when people discuss slavery is American chattel slavery (McGary and Lawson 1992, 8–9). However, this form of slavery differs from other forms of slavery (e.g., slavery in ancient Greece) in an important way. Chattel slaves were viewed as objects or things that could be bought or sold or used in any other way that their slaveowners saw fit. The slave owners thought that these slaves had no right to have their desires and wishes acknowledged, let alone respected, by them. Any limitations placed on the slaveowner's treatment of slaves was not because of any rights the slaves possessed, but because of how such treatment was perceived by slave owners to effect their interests. Viewing chattel slaves as property is quite different from simply placing a value or a monetary value on human life. Some tort lawyers make handsome livings by determining how much compensation should be given for the loss of life and limb. However, in doing so, they are not viewing their clients as property or things without rights or valuable interests.

In a letter to Henry C. Wright in 1846, Frederick Douglass (1999, 51) gives the following characterization of the slave redemption efforts of fellow abolitionists:

> Every man has a natural and inalienable right to himself. The inference from this is, "that man cannot hold property in man"—and as man cannot hold property in man, neither can Hugh Auld nor the United States have any right of property in me, they have no right to sell me—and, having no right to sell me, no one has a right to buy me.

According to Douglass, the best reason for thinking that abolitionists should not purchase the freedom of slaves is that you cannot rightfully sell something that you don't own. And, given that slaves are human beings, slaveowners cannot sell something they don't rightfully own. On the other side of the equation, abolitionists cannot rightfully purchase slaves, because they cannot buy something from someone who does not have the right to sell it. Douglass has given us a convincing argument for the conclusion that purchasing slaves should not be seen as a market exchange.

These considerations force us to re-conceptualize our problem. Is it right to think of redemption as involving slaves being bought? Perhaps a better way of describing what the slave redeemers are doing would be ransoming slaves rather than purchasing them. Suppose we view the slave redemption efforts in the Sudan as a kind of ransom. Should this

The intuition that I am drawing on here is the belief that it is never morally permissible to reward people for intentional wrongdoing. Of course, there are often good consequentialist reasons for following this principle. However, my point is not to give those reasons. My intuition is that we have reason to follow this principle even when the consequences of not doing so outweigh those for doing so. Obviously, some people disagree. Even amongst people who believe that certain things (like lying) should be forbidden, there is strong disagreement over the method or principles that should be used to identify an actual list of duties and rights.

A very common method is one that I have employed. It relies on the moral intuitions of the parties involved in the moral disputes. Moral intuitions are clearly valuable, but this method for deciding what we ought to do has not withstood close scrutiny. The discomfort with relying on moral intuitions has not led philosophers to reject them, but instead to try to find a way to refine them. John Rawls developed a method to specify the content of a deontological theory by refining our moral intuitions. He called it the method of reflective equilibrium (1971, 48–51). The method of reflective equilibrium involves working back and forth between our considered moral judgments about a particular case, the principles that apply to the case, and the reasons that bear on accepting these principles, and revising our cases and principles whenever necessary to achieve coherence. This, of course, is only one method that has been offered for refining our moral intuitions. Kant, of course, provided us with another method. However, the methods offered by Kant and Rawls have not convinced consequentialists.

Slave redemptions don't simply allow wrongdoers to avoid punishment and the payment of compensation for their wrongful acts; they also allow wrongdoers to be paid for their vices! This fact provides potential wrongdoers with an additional motive for failing to do what they ought to do. We could attempt to avoid these outcomes by embracing the Platonic view that "justice is its own reward." But, unfortunately, this response is not available to the consequentialist because she is more likely than not to adopt the incentives or sanctions models of moral motivation. On these models, people do what they ought to do because they want to be rewarded for doing so or they want to avoid the negative consequences of their moral failings. Since this is the case, consequentialists must be concerned about any program that provides people with additional motives for doing wrong.

One might think that the NRW principle should never be violated because it always respects rights. And since deontological moral systems define rights in nonderivative terms, we have a nonconsequentialist reason for not violating the principle. However, with cases of slave redemptions

If one does not violate these rules, then one follows them impartially in regard to everyone in the relevant group. How does this apply to the issue of slave redemption in the Sudan? A deontologist could argue that given that there is not enough money to buy the freedom of all the persons held as slaves, showing partiality by purchasing some slaves violates the principle of impartiality and the agent-neutral perspective held so dearly by deontologists.

There are good reasons for thinking that the slave redeemers in the Sudan show partiality. For example, it has been alleged that Christian groups are more likely to redeem persons who are sympathetic to their religious views. And clearly, in the case of family members who redeem members of their family, there is partiality. Of course, one could try to argue that family loyalties and commitments don't violate the principles of impartiality. Frederick Douglass raises this concern in the letter that I quoted from above. Douglass rejected the idea that he should purchase his freedom, but he thought it was permissible for friends to do so. Douglass (1999, 53) said:

> I am free to say, that, had I possessed one hundred and fifty pounds, I would have seen Hugh Auld kicking, before I would have given it to him. I would have waited until till the emergency came, and only given up the money when nothing else would do. But my friends thought it best to provide against the contingency; they acted on their own responsibility, and I am not disturbed about the results.

In John Stauffer's paper in this volume, he discusses Douglass's concern with the belief that it is all right to have someone else pay ransom money to purchase your freedom, but unacceptable to do so yourself. According to Stauffer, Frederick Douglass also chided another ex-slave, John Douglass, for purchasing the freedom of his mother. The only sense that I can make of Frederick Douglass's reluctance, or in some cases, straight-out rejection, of slaves purchasing their own freedom or the freedom of members of their own families, is something like an impartiality principle.

In the Sudan, then, we want to insure that the people who are being purchased are not beneficiaries of partial treatment. In practice that might be harder to do than in theory. But, at least, it is not clear that purchasing slaves in the Sudan must violate the impartiality requirement. If it can be done in a way that does not, then we can't use this as a general reason to forbid it, especially when it promotes good consequences.

Virtue Ethics and the Problem of Slave Redemptions

Although I don't have an apriori argument in hand, in the light of the above considerations, when all is said and done, I doubt that we can give

Virtues are paramount in this ethical perspective, but not the exclusive focus of someone doing virtue ethics. The virtues are usually seen as stable character traits (such as honesty, generosity, and courage) that generate good lives. The virtues are important, but the person doing virtue ethics is also concerned about understanding how vices and other shortcomings affect our lives. Although virtues are the important focus, we need to be clear here. Deontologists and consequentialists can also focus on virtues, but when they do they see them as stable dispositions to act according to duty. A true eudaimonist theory does not see dutifulness as a necessary condition for a good life. But as I alluded to above, there are varied accounts of virtue ethics. Some of these accounts are not eudaimonist.

Perhaps the following example will help to illustrate the difference between theories that make duties primary and ones that do not. A common complaint today is that doctors know very little about their patients and that too many don't care enough about their patients and are not prone to make sacrifices for them. Some people attribute the present state of the doctor-patient relationship to the understanding of this relationship in terms of rights and duties. The critics believe that seeing things in terms of rights and duties will encourage people to fall short of being the best that they can be. Of course, the supporters of understanding the doctor-patient relationship in terms of rights and duties would argue there are good reasons why this model has become so prevalent. The model is seen as necessary in order to protect both parties from abuse. Even doctors who see themselves as acting in the interest of their patients can inadvertently cause abuse. The issue of medical paternalism is taken to be an illustration of this fact and as a good reason for preserving the rights and duties model of the doctor-patient relationship.

However, one group of virtue ethicists would respond that the rights and duties model in the case above fails to give a central place to virtues like care and concern for others, patience, and self-sacrifice. Writers like Annette Baier (1985, especially chapters 6 and 12) have claimed that there is a tendency to ignore these virtues, and by doing so, we are unable to capture a central aspect of what it means to be moral. Baier's criticism is not restricted to theorists who focus on rights and duties. She is well aware that even some virtue ethicists may omit these virtues. They may do so because these virtues are usually exemplified by women and people without power and influence. The paternalism counterexample fails to appreciate that in the real world people are very often not in relationships where personal autonomy can be given the highest priority.

Is there an analogous case for how our concerns about the ethics of slave redemption in the Sudan might best be understood? Would we fare better by not looking at this issue in terms of rights and duties?

Chapter Twelve

The Next Best Thing

MARTIN BUNZL

Let us assume that the arguments of Karlan and Krueger that appear in this volume are correct. That is to say, let us assume that redeeming the freedom of one slave (under most circumstances) does no harm and likely does at least some good. That is to say, let us assume that if I buy the freedom of 10 slaves, no more than 10 people will be newly enslaved and likely less than 10 will be enslaved. So, all other things being equal, net-net, let us assume that I do more good than harm. (All of these assumptions bracket deontic objections taken up by others in this volume.) Well, so what, Peter Singer might say—you can bring about a much greater good by giving your money to feed starving people. (In fact that is just what Singer has said [in conversation] about this issue.) I want to examine the force of this prescription in what follows. In other words, I am interested in the question of to what degree our actions in helping others should be constrained by the fact that we might be able to do more or better. I am going to be especially interested in focusing on the force of the phrase "might be able to" and in contrasting it to what we are likely to do. The core question I am interested in, specific to the subject of this volume, is this: at least when it comes to doing good, as in the act of freeing a slave, even if there are alternatives that would produce greater good, what kinds of factors might undermine the likelihood of those alternatives being realized? That is a quick and dirty version of the question that I am interested in. The more proper version is comparative: at least when it comes to doing good, as in the act of freeing a slave, even if there are alternatives that would produce greater good, what kind of factors might undermine the comparative likelihood of those alternatives being realized over the likelihood of freeing a slave? One more twist, for we ought to worry not just that the best alternative is less likely to be realized than the second best, but that that comparative likelihood is relatively hard to change: at least when it comes to doing good, as in the act of freeing a slave, even if there are alternatives that would produce greater good, how robust are the factors that might diminish the comparative likelihood of those alternatives being realized over the likelihood of freeing a slave?

Let us assume that to be the case without worrying too much why it might be the case. Any of the three routes to that conclusion I have suggested above will do.

But to stop here is to stop far short of the finishing line if our goal is to achieve *action* that instantiates such a "greatest good" general principle. Let us consider some of the ways in which a smooth and seamless transition from a greatest good prescription to action may break down. If we view decisions as being made on a case-by-case basis, the most obvious of these are epistemic and temporal. I may not be able to know which is the best alternative, and even if I were able to know it in principle, the time it would take to find out carries costs that need to be offset against the benefits. These are the standard objections that motivate the transformation of a greatest good principle from being a moral case-by-case guide into a moral guide for formulating rules to govern classes of cases—like, in general, greater good will come from feeding the starving than freeing slaves. But, on either variant, there is a traditional worry about whether a greatest good principle will in fact produce the greatest good that goes all the way back to Sidgwick. We would not need a moral code in the first place if we were not prone to act immorally or at least amorally. One who advocates a moral code against this background on the grounds that it will produce the greatest good, if followed, has to off-set these benefits with the costs of implementing such a policy—costs which may be high depending on the state of nature that forms its backdrop. But that assumes success in transforming us whatever the costs. Sidgwick's concern was what the consequences are if no full transformation is possible, if some of our natural inclinations are intractable and not fully reformable (Sidgwick 1907).

Sidgwick's worries arise from the tension between those we are close to and strangers. By his lights, promoting the general good and the relations of "affection" we have to those close to us will come into conflict. You might think that in response, "Utilitarianism must therefore prescribe such a culture of feelings as will, so far as possible, counteract this tendency" (Sidgwick 1907, 434). But the problem is whether we can do so without transforming such feelings into "a watery kindness" (as Sidwick points out, the phrase comes from Aristotle) when it is expressed in its universalized form. Better, Sidgwick thinks, to pay the price of giving up a degree of impartiality to harness feelings for the other in their full strength at least at the parochial level.

I think this picture of thinking and feeling is at best only part of the story. Of course we have special feelings for those close to us as compared to strangers. But it is not as if strangers don't evoke feelings in us as well. It is not that we lack a culture of feeling toward them. Worse, ignoring that emotional dimension of our relations to others feeds the illusion that

ments between random pairings of the previously exposed stimuli and novel ones (both of which were irregular octagons), a statistically significant preference for the previously exposed stimuli was demonstrated. (Sixteen of 24 subjects preferred the old stimuli to the novel ones but only five of the 24 recognized them.) Kunst-Wilson and Zajonc used these data to argue that we have the capacity to make judgments noncognitively, and their research has become central to a debate about whether cognitive representation is a necessary condition for emotional responses to stimuli. The conclusion I want to draw is different and twofold: first, familiarity affects preferences. But more importantly, familiarity starts much further from home than we might think—even in the domain of what is, for all intents and purposes, the unfamiliar. As a result, any pairwise choice situation may be directly subject to preference effects without our even knowing it. Still, someone might object as follows—we are discussing familiarity as an adjunct to moral reasoning. Surely when I ask you to choose who is most deserving, A or B, that you may prefer A over B, even without knowing it, is not necessarily to say that your moral choice will be affected.

But even if mere familiarity did not have such direct effects, it can also have indirect effects in a circumstance of moral choice as well in virtue of its effects on empathy. For it is a truism that empathy is shaped (in part) by preferences. And if mere familiarity can drive preferences, then it will do so as well when it comes to empathy. The news here is not that, but rather that if the effects of familiarity are so fine-grained that they can be exercised on choices between strangers, so too will they differentially affect our empathy for strangers. Of course feeling empathy for a stranger would be a gain to the extent that we view empathy as an unalloyed virtue. But, at least as an adjunct to moral reasoning, judgments of fairness turn out to be biased by empathy whether or not familiarity and its associated preferences bias such judgments directly.

Traditionally, empathy has been viewed as a necessary condition on prosocial behavior. You walk down the street and see a stranger who needs your help. Standard social psychology analyzes this sort of prima facie other-directed behavior as a function of the perceived opportunity costs you face and the degree of empathy you feel. (For example, Sears et al. 1985.) It is for that reason (among others) that educational efforts to motivate and increase empathic responses are taken to serve a social good. But Batson and his colleagues (Batson et al. 1995) have shown that inducing empathy is a double-edged sword when it comes to determining whom to help as opposed to whether they will be helped. Batson and his colleagues deceived student subjects into thinking they were participating in an experiment to assess the consequences of positive versus negative consequences on workers (among other things). Students believed they

is realizable but weak, but rather that it is subject to catastrophic failure under circumstances when it would be most needed if it were to be relied on as an adjunct to moral reasoning.

Before proceeding, readers may wish to go to: *http://fas-philosophy .rutgers.edu/~bunzl/slavery.html*. You will find some pictures at that site. Please view them in the context of a thought experiment in which you receive a direct mail solicitation or a solicitation on the street to support efforts to combat hunger in country x. You are told that these pictures illustrate the kind of population that will be served. Now click through to the pictures, viewing set 1 first and then set 2. In each case gauge your reactions. If you have decided to proceed as outlined above, don't read on until you have done so.

A word to those readers who elected not to go to the website above. The site contains two sets of pictures of undernourished children. The first set are of children who are clearly underweight, gaunt, and sad-looking. The second set are of children who are more dramatically emaciated and who appear to be near death.

If you did look at the site, how did you react and how did you feel? Here is how I suspect you responded. The first set of pictures probably evoked feelings of sadness in you, and if not empathy (since the pictures are of children and you [presumably] are an adult), sympathy. That empathy or sympathy may have been followed by a feeling that you wished you could do something to help these sorts of children. In the case of the second set of pictures, I suspect you also felt sadness, even extreme sadness and sorrow. But at the same time, you probably felt anxiety and some distress. You may have literally sucked in air and physically recoiled from the screen, possibly averting your eyes. If you forced your gaze to linger, your feelings of distress likely increased and you may have been aware of a feeling of physical disgust. You may have had the same kind of feeling if you have ever seen pictures of a decaying corpse. If you had that feeling of disgust, you most likely will have broken your gaze and averted your eyes. Whether you felt distress and stopped looking or your feeling reached a level of disgust immediately or after looking for a while, I suspect you *felt* less empathy or sympathy for the second set of children than you did for the first even as you may have thought they were more deserving of your sympathy. If I am right, you also did not have a feeling that you wished you could do something to help these sorts of children— your level of distress and (if it happened) disgust reaction trumped that. If you had such a reaction, note how it distanced you from your connection to the pictures. You may not only have jolted back from the screen, but psychologically, you may have caught yourself thinking that you did not want to see these images, or thinking that I had a lot of nerve to have you look at them, or having a myriad of other self-focused thoughts.

stimuli. It is hard to discuss this without some indelicacy—but think of your own experience when it comes to defecating. Like most people you probably examine the results of your efforts on a daily basis. And if you are like most people, your nose wrinkles every time you do so. One would think that after so many years of following this procedure, you would have gotten used to it. But if you are like me, the wrinkle of your nose, the recoil of your body is as robust today as it was when you were seven years old. And it is not just so with fecal matter. Other disgust reactions are remarkable for their hold on us even in the face of countervailing considerations of rationality. Take spit. When you kiss another, you don't mind exchanging spit. Yet the idea of drinking a teaspoon of that same person's spit is profoundly off-putting. These are examples of the hold that so-called basic emotions have on us. Maybe there is no such thing as a basic emotion, but even if there isn't, disgust prompted by these sorts of emotions lacks much of the cultural overlay that disgust at the idea of having sex with a sibling presumably has. Disgust with such a cultural overlay also shows remarkable persistence. I hesitate to recommend you try sleeping with your siblings to see if it gets any less off-putting with repetition. Try this instead: find a dead cockroach and sterilize it. Now put it in your mouth. Repeat the effort once a day for a week and see how far you get. Or, if you prefer, go to your local hospital supply store and buy a new bedpan. Unwrap it and pour some wine into it. Drink the wine if you can. Repeat the procedure every day for a week and see if you feel any less reluctant about the exercise. (Most of the above is inspired by Paul Rozin's work [see for example Rozin and Nemeroff 1990].) Even imagining some disgusting acts has quite robust consequences. Want to diminish your desire for bagels? Take a bagel out of your fridge and now just *imagine* a dead cockroach lying between the two halves. Now try to eat it and see how you feel. (Do you think you will feel an overwhelming need to check that there is no cockroach there before you eat it? And even if there is none there, will a feeling of nausea at the idea of its being there persist?)

Of course some people do not have these reactions. Whether they don't as a matter of accommodation or preexisting disposition is an open question. Perhaps they were never put off by these things in the first place. Or more likely, unlike me (and most likely, you) they are capable of becoming desensitized over the long run by a disposition that they have and we lack. But, be that as it may, our concern is with the role of disgust response for most of us, and most of us have disgust responses that are remarkable in their strength and persistence over time.

When it comes to familiarity, things are much more complicated and murky. If the incidence of disgust is easy to identify but our reactions are hard to purge, the situation of familiarity at best runs in the other

when subjects are viewing the images with an assigned task that calls for social individuation.)

If the truly needy are unfamiliar (in the way discussed above) and disgust-provoking in their very neediness, then empathy comes under attack from both directions and its chances of prevailing in provoking action will suffer. But even bracketing these external disruptions to our empathic capacities, empathy itself contains the seeds of its own destruction. If you were like me in your reaction to the second set of images of starving children discussed above, *both* distress and disgust functioned to break your connection with the needs of the children, replacing it with your own needs. So far we have only discussed the disgust component. If altruism has empathy as a necessary condition, it is not just any empathy, but empathy for or with the distress of the other. I experience what you feel. My feelings match yours. Whether I respond to those feelings on your behalf or mine is a second question. On Martin Hoffman's view (2000) my capacity to have a sympathetic reaction to such empathic distress eventually gets replaced by a self-directed reaction when the empathic distress reaches a certain level (which is what the images were designed to elicit). Empathy draws us to others, but if we get too drawn to them and their condition is too extreme, our other-directed response turns to a focus on ourselves and withdrawal from the other. Thus the greater your distress, and my empathic response to it, the greater the chance that I will react on my behalf, not yours. If that is right then, if the neediest are the most deserving (because helping them will do the greatest good), they will be more likely to prompt a self-directed response as compared to the less deserving.

For distress reactions, unlike disgust reactions, there is no reason not to think that the tipping point from concern for the other to concern for oneself is quite varied and subject to many determinants. Be that as it may, with the exception of Mother Teresa, for most of us, moral prescription and empathic responses will part ways at some point. Here a moral prescriptivist would do well to think like a preacher. A preacher, at least one interested in producing good, ought to worry about whether his or her prescriptions fall within the realm of psychological possibility for his or her charges. That is not to say that there are not religious orders that render us always wanting. But a religion that makes the task of moral improvement hopelessly unattainable runs the risk of provoking the embrace of sin—after all, if we are doomed to be sinners, why not at least have fun along the way?

Of course the danger, for a preacher or prescriptivist, or temptation (depending on your view) is to misjudge psychological possibility. If aiming too high makes us all and only sinners, aiming too low makes it too easy for us to be saints.

tions) comes close to this sort of impossibility. For even in the case of disgust, we have allowed that some people are capable of overriding their disgust reactions (most notably, Catherine of Siena; see William Miller 1997).

So, am I driven back to calculational opportunism as the only reason to advocate advocating second best? Is that the only reason to prescribe freeing slaves over feeding the hungry? To do so is to accept the picture as one that sees the matter as respecting our agency or behaving opportunistically. But that seems to me to set up a false dichotomy. The tradition of moral reasoning begun by Piaget and developed by Kohlberg treats (nearly) all of us as capable of moral reasoning with varying degrees of sophistication. But in addition to its disinterest in the consequences of such reasoning for moral action, it treats moral reasoning as a process that is isolated from the effects of other psychological process. The whole enterprise is a purely internal matter. We tend to treat agency as an artifact of this reasoning process, and emotion as an interference—what Elster terms "sand in the machine." That picture feeds the idea that with discipline we can filter out that interference. But what if that is an illusion? Some (like Peter Railton 1984) would turn this into a virtue, arguing that it is a hopeless enterprise for us to hope to follow the dictates of consequentialism directly and explicitly. Instead, we should aim to harness our psychology. "A sophisticated act-consequentialist should realize that certain goods are reliably attainable—or attainable at all—only if people have well developed characters; that the human psyche is capable of only so much self-regulation and refinement; and that human perception and reasoning are liable to a host of biases and errors. Therefore individuals may be more likely to act rightly if they possess certain enduring motivational patterns, character traits, or *prima facie* commitments to rules in addition to what whatever commitment they have to act for the best" (1984, 158).

But, whether you view agency expansively as encompassing these emotions, or narrowly but as always operating with them in the background, understanding their vagaries, plasticity, and educability is unavoidable if we are interested in understanding our capacity for moral action. Only then can we know if the next best thing is the most we can reasonably be expected to do.

Bibliography

Batson, C. Daniel, Tricia Klein, Lori Highberger, and Laura Shaw (1995), "Immorality From Empathy-Induced Altruism: When Compassion and Justice Conflict," *Journal of Personality and Social Psychology* 68(6): 1042–1054.

Chapter Thirteen _____

What's Wrong with Slavery?

KWAME ANTHONY APPIAH

I grew up in Ghana's Ashanti region, in its capital, Kumasi, which was, for more than two centuries, beginning in the late 1600s, the center of the flourishing Asante empire. At some point in my education (I don't remember how early) I learned that the kingdom of Asante had been the center of a great trading system, with roads radiating out from the capital in every direction, connecting us, for example, with the coast and the Atlantic trading system, and with the north and the trans-Saharan trade. Gold, everyone knew, was one of the commodities we exported: the empire of Asante covered most of what was once called the Gold Coast (and became the British Gold Coast Colony and then, at independence in 1957, Ghana). And we imported weapons, I knew, beginning with guns supplied through the Dutch and Danish and European castles on the coast, including Christiansborg Castle in Accra, finished in 1661 by the Danes, just a few years before the first Asante king, Osei Tutu, began his rise to power. (The ancient guns now carried by Asante soldiers on ceremonial occasions today are called "Dane guns" in much of English-speaking West Africa.) What I don't remember hearing much about was the centrality of the slave trade to the growth of the Asante empire in the eighteenth century. As plantation slavery expanded in the New World through the eighteenth century the demand for slave labor grew enormously. At the start of the eighteenth century as much as two-thirds of the value of Asante trade was in slaves. By the late eighteenth century 100,000 slaves a year were leaving Africa's western coasts for the Americas, many of them through the forty or so British, Danish, and Dutch forts along the Gold Coast. When the British banned the North Atlantic slave trade in the early nineteenth century, Asante expanded its trade in kola nuts (whose role in West African social life was somewhere between that of coffee and that of alcohol in the modern United States). But the suppression of the slave trade began the period of imperial decline, which was to end with final conquest by the British at the start of the twentieth century.

Ironically, however, while the slave trade played an important role in the consolidation of Asante power, it was probably the importation of

(Perbi 2004, 3). After all, a chief might refer to his subjects as his children, as well: in each case, however, the point was to focus on a reciprocal, though unequal, relationship, in which the superior had responsibilities for the welfare of the subordinate as well as a right of command, and the subordinate had duties of obedience to the master or mistress, but also rights against him or her to maintenance—to food, clothing, and shelter. An *akoa* would also have had other rights: in particular, to marriage and to life. In every Akan community only a chief had the right to kill someone, and then only for an offense; and a master who engaged in adultery with his *akoa*'s wife was (at least in theory) as liable to the penalties for adultery as anyone else.

An *akoa* was not a chattel, a possession. While you could, no doubt, send servants to work for someone else for a period, you could not transfer them to anyone else without their consent (or that of their families). There was another kind of subordinate person in many households, an *awowa*, whose presence was the result of an economic transaction: an *awowa* was a member of someone else's family who was sent to work for you in return for a loan, and who remained until the loan was repaid. (The usual translation of *awowa* is "pawn.") But a pawn was not strictly a possession either. You couldn't sell her because, of course, she was due to be returned to her family once the debt was repaid.

There were two other kinds of subordinates in many Asante households, who might have been called "slaves." One was the *dommum* or war captive. Such captives might, if they were lucky, be redeemed by the payment of a ransom. But if they were not redeemed, they were obliged to work for and obey their captors: and, in the end, they might be sold. The other was the *donko*, whom you would most naturally call a slave. The *donko* had been bought, or could be sold, in a slave market. Some had become slaves under the law or custom of some other state and had been bought by Asantes; some were the children of existing slaves; and some had been captured in warfare or raiding and not been redeemed.

A final sort of subordinate, who could be found at work especially in the households of chiefs, was the *akyere*. This was someone who had been found guilty of a capital offense and condemned to death. (Since there were no prisons in Asante—though there were regions of towns set aside for the residence of such condemned people—the main forms of punishment were fines and corporal and capital punishment.) Such people were not executed immediately on sentencing. Rather they were compelled to do what they were ordered to do through the authority of the chief who had condemned them until such time as it was deemed religiously auspicious to kill them. When a king died, for example, many of these condemned people would be executed to "accompany" him to the next life. Or they might be executed as an offering to a god to insure its

from that town. It is only recently that it has occurred to me that this matters to him, not just because he is, no doubt, concerned, as Asantes tend to be, with a proper accounting of his origins, but also because his family, unlike most of those in the village, never belonged to anyone. The low status of these slave ancestors still matters, then, generations after slavery has gone.

Even though the sale of slaves is illegal and demands for unpaid work are unenforceable, there are still people, descended probably from either a *dommum* or a *donko,* who work in the households of prosperous Asantes without remuneration. (There are also some who are sent by families that cannot afford to feed them, people who are properly servants, *nkoa*, though their remuneration is not monetary, and the families to which they go tend to treat them like the poor relation in a Victorian novel.)[2] Their status, so it seems to me, is like that of children. They are in the care of the families they work for, which have obligations to maintain and support them, but their labor and their lives are pretty much governed by the wills of the people in whose households they live. They are a kind of fictive kin, if you like, but they are not social equals. In principle, they are free to leave whenever they choose. In practice, they often have nowhere to go. Never having been paid, they have no savings. Often they have only the most basic education, so their only skill is domestic work, a market in which there is a great deal of competition.

Once, when I was a child, I asked my father, in a room full of people, how we were related to a woman whom I knew and liked, who lived in one of the family houses. I thought of her, in fact, as one of my "aunts." My father brushed the question angrily aside. Only later, when we were alone, did he say that one should never inquire after people's ancestry in public. She was, as it turned out, the descendant of a family slave. Everybody in the family knew this, and that meant that she was of lower status than the rest of us. As children we were required to be courteous to all adults, even those of lower status. But that didn't mean they weren't inferior.

I am not here reporting my father's thoughts or mine about this woman's status. My father was trying to avoid embarrassing her; he almost certainly did not think her ancestry an embarrassment himself. But she was often treated by people I knew in ways that reflected a conception of her as having an inferior status. And I suspect that the most important truth here is that this is how she thought of herself. She could not be sold, like her ancestors; she could not be separated against her will from her children; she was free to work wherever she could and live wherever it pleased her. But she would never think of herself as equal to

[2] *Nkoa* is the plural of *akoa.*

of slavery, and, especially when slaves are expensive, it is not likely to be common. But to say this is not to defend the institution (as the paternalists wrongly believed). For the lives of the happiest slaves, men and women well treated by their masters, are still diminished by their status. And at the heart of the matter, so it seems to me, are two issues: hereditary social inferiority and heteronomous personal life. I want in the rest of this essay to explain something of the character of these harms, and argue that freeing someone from the legal status of a slave does not guarantee that you will solve either of them. Emancipation is important, but undoing the harms of slavery is, I think, slow work.

The differential treatment of blacks and whites in the United States before emancipation simply presupposed the inferior status of black people. Certainly slaves were legally inferior in social status: they were expected to display deference to others, and if they failed to do so—if they were "uppity"—they could be punished for it. But it was because they were black that they could be enslaved, and even free blacks were usually treated as inferior to white people of the same wealth or accomplishments. White people could be Mr. and Mrs. Smith; black people were Jim and Jemima. Black people were expected to let white people precede them through doorways, to step out of their way on the sidewalk, to walk past them with heads bowed, to avoid looking them in the eye. These rules largely applied, as I say, to free blacks as well, before the Civil War.

One way of understanding this fact is to suppose that even free blacks were stigmatized because, though they were legally free, they belonged, unlike white people, to a kind of people that could be enslaved. There was, in other words, an intimate connection between racial disrespect and slave status—a nexus nicely captured in the Fifteenth Amendment to the United States Constitution that says that voting rights may not be abridged on account of "race, color, or previous condition of servitude." Being a Negro, having a dark skin, being a slave, were easily conflated in the American system. More than this, because slaves were inferior, their work was stigmatized, too: agricultural labor, associated with deferential, dependent slaves, was something that respectable people did not do. It is noticeable that that association has survived. White people who do the sort of work the slaves used to do, working all day in the hot sun, get sunburn on their necks. Their necks are red; and "redneck" is not a term of respect.

Notice that the law played a relatively small role in defining the patterns of deference required of the slave. An owner's right to punish a slave was a matter of law; treating a white person, even a social inferior, this way would, from a legal point of view, have been assault and battery. Deference was enforced not so much by legal punishment as by a social

to have self-respect; and to maintain this confidence, he thought, it was necessary that the institutions of the state should reflect back to one an image of oneself as a dignified person deserving of respect. This psychological claim is extremely plausible. It is one of the great wrongs that racism, sexism, and homophobia have all inflicted that they have created a society that reflects back to black people, women, and lesbians and gays a demeaning image of themselves that is an obstacle to self-respect. As Charles Taylor has insisted, it is precisely this active debasement of people on the basis of their race, nationality, sexual orientation, class, or gender, that has fueled the "politics of recognition" that has come to be so dominant in modern societies. People who are treated with social contempt recognize that they are being wronged and demand the fundamental respect whose denial they understand has made self-respect difficult for them.

Slavery as a social or legal institution has built into it, in other words, a denial of the social bases of self-respect: it defines the slave as lower in status precisely by denying that she has a plan of life worthy of consideration and rejecting the enslaved person's claim to manage her own life. Some slaves, as Frederick Douglass demonstrated vividly, sustain self-respect in a society that denies them respect. (So too, women in sexist societies may know that they live lives worth living and have plans that they are entitled to pursue, even when most people around them think that their lives need managing for them.) But the experience of enslavement and servitude makes this very difficult. And placing this obstacle to self-respect in a person's way does her a very great wrong.

It does her wrong, of course, whether it is done by the state or by society without legal sanction. And that is why, when slavery as a legal institution is abolished, there is no guarantee that the wrong will cease. We have seen this over and over again in post-emancipation societies historically, as I have already pointed out. And so it is not surprising that the end of slavery is only the beginning of real freedom.

So much for an outline of the first of slavery's major offenses against the enslaved: its imposition of a low status with the consequent denial of the social bases of self-respect. The second, associated wrong, as I say, is that slavery imposes heteronomy on people. Instead of allowing them to manage their own lives, it allows the slaveholder to shape the slave's life entirely without regard to her concerns. The denial of the social bases of respect undermines one's belief in one's capacity to run one's own life; the imposition of heteronomy denies one the exercise of that capacity.

It is central to human flourishing that each of us should be master of our own fate; we have ultimate responsibility for our own lives and the right to make the major decisions. Those decisions, properly made, will acknowledge the moral interests of others, so that mastering my fate

Appendix: "They Call Us Animals," Testimonies of Abductees and Slaves in Sudan

JOK MADUT JOK

Introduction

The resurgence and practice of slavery in Sudan between 1983 and 2001, although built upon the old racial, social, and economic foundations of nineteenth-century slavery, was triggered this time around by the on-going north-south conflict (Idris 2001; Collins 1992; Johnson 2002). The government used it to achieve two goals at the same time. It allowed the government to arm and train the militias that were also used to fight the war by proxy. It also functioned as a way to appease the Arab tribes of Darfur and Kordofan, which would have otherwise been hostile to the government in Khartoum for its neglect of these areas in terms of social services. The result has been that southern women and children have been abducted and taken into slavery in the north and subjected to various fates. Women are used for physical labor in farming, as domestic servants, and as sexual slaves. Large numbers of women have been found to have performed vital labor for Arab farmers and herdsmen over this period. Women have also been useful to the slaveowners biologically as well as ideologically. Biologically, their reproductive potential has proven one of the reasons for the persistence of this practice, as many Arab families make claims to children born to these women during their captivity. Ideologically, these slave women serve as the means with which to reconfigure race relations in order to forge a homogeneous society based on Arab and Islamic identity. Southern women are to be found throughout Darfur and Kordofan, as forced and free laborers, as concubines and wives, and as internally displaced persons and migrant workers. Children, both abductees and those born in captivity, are also found in these conditions in the north. This appendix attempts to describe what life looks like for these slave women and children. This is done through testimonies from some of the women and young adults who were once enslaved but managed to escape or were released otherwise.

Years ago, when I was doing research for a book on slavery in Sudan (Jok 2001), I traveled all over Bahr el-Ghazal, the southern Sudan's region most affected by slave raiding. Since 1999, I have undertaken ten trips to the region, six of them related to a project aimed at making a registry of cooking, cultivation, tending animals in the desert, collecting firewood, fetching water from the wells, washing cloths, and other domestic chores. Domestic servants report being made to sleep in the kitchen, while the cattle tenders are made to sleep in the same space as the cattle. They also report various other forms of abuse such as being addressed with demeaning terms like *Abd*, "slave." Women's and girls' testimonies cite rape, forced "marriage," and other sexual abuses amounting, in certain cases, to sexual slavery. Many of those who were freed were either pregnant or gave birth to children fathered by their captors. In some cases, women were freed and instructed to return to the South but leaving the children behind with the Arab men who fathered them.

Atem Garang Akol, who was abducted at a very young age, and had worked for his captor Muhammed Juma, spoke of witnessing many children being sold to the Kababish who live further up in North and West Darfur. He also spoke in detail about his duties during the many years of his captivity. He had been promised by his master that he would not be treated like a slave and that he would be paid for grazing duties he was performing. His payment was one cow paid to him annually. He was told to keep his cows together with the master's and that he would have the exclusive use of their dairy products, but he was prevented from selling the cows or taking them away, which really means that they were not his cattle, and therefore in reality, he was not being paid for his work. Speaking about his master, he said:

> When I was first turned over to him by the people who had captured me, he had told me that I should not fear him and that I would be treated just like one of his children. He said that being asked to do things around the house or to graze cattle was not to enslave me, but rather to share the tasks with the other boys, his sons, and this seemed to have been the case for the first ten days, after which everybody else in his house began to be really mean and calling me names such as *abd* or *jengai*, the black one, the donkey, or the dog. This is when everyone began to order me around. Even the other kids whom I had been told would do the same chores as myself were now sending me to serve them. When I would go grazing with them, they would go and sit under the shade of the brush and shout at me that I should go and round up the cattle.... They threatened me with violence.... They said they could simply kill me right in the forest and go home to tell their family that I had escaped and nobody would question them. I was always terrified. I had seen other boys and girls subjected to terrible cruelty and I dared not risk becoming like those children. I did everything as I was told and that is how I was able to survive. In fact I think he began to think that I had forgotten where I had come from. But the

clothes; he wore rags, and his face was always so downcast that he made me not want to look at his eyes when he spoke during the few times that I would go visit him in his barn. . . . He made me feel so bad about him. At times I even felt much better off despite my own miserable futureless existence. . . . It is so strange how one becomes immune to pain when you have not known much else all your childhood."

Another returned abductee I interviewed, a young woman whose master had renamed her Zeinab, had the following to say:

> The man in whose house I had worked for a few months following my abduction was nice at first, but when he decided one day to force himself onto me he would not stop anymore and there was nothing I could do as he told me that he would tell his other friends to rape me if I did not comply with his demands. He demanded that I become his wife, but he had no courage to tell his real wife and did not want his neighbors to know about it. His wife still found out and she became furious but aimed her anger at me instead. She would not stop yelling all kinds of insults at me and threatened to kill me, at which point the husband decided to let me go because it was going to bring disgrace to him. At this time I was already two months pregnant. I moved to a displaced persons camp in el-Daein where I met up with other Dinka people from my home area. I remained there for nearly five years, and that is where the CEAWAC people found me and told me they could take me home if I wanted to. Although my child is an Arab child, I consider him my compensation. I am blessed that my child was not taken away like all the other women who were forced to have children with Arab men and were forced again to leave the children behind.

Many similar stories abound: children who have reported serious physical abuse to the police only to end up in police detention instead of their cases being investigated; girls who have been sexually abused by a father and his sons; children who feel forced to remain in captivity because they do not know where they would go if they escape. Other stories are about escape from bondage, the journey back to the south, hunger and thirst along the rough terrain between towns in Kordofan and Darfur and the river Kir. The picture that emerges from these stories is one of total despair; but one that does not diminish the thirst and quest for freedom. And freedom, whatever disappointments await one at the end of the escape tunnel, is worth every bit of sacrifice, the slaves say.

Akuol Majok, a 27-year-old mother of a four-year-old girl, was abducted from the village of Mabok Tong in northern Bahr el-Ghazal in 1998. Her daughter was fathered by one of her captors. She was now a free woman, as she had been released through her family's efforts to redeem her. She was pregnant with her second child when we interviewed

grain, provide health care, and interview people about their future aspirations regarding a possibility of return home. Everything would look as normal as a refugee could be. At night, however, it is a different story. The camps are swarmed by security agents to interrogate and arrest anyone they would have noticed talking to the foreigners during the daytime. The Arab Baggara would also send groups of armed men to confiscate the relief supplies distributed earlier to the refugees and abductees. All the food, especially grain, is looted and people beaten. This food gets used to hire some of us to work for the Arabs to clear planting fields and to serve in their homes as servants. The supplies that were supposed to go to us are confiscated and are used to enslave us with. They sing songs about these activities. One song is about how to use the Khawaja [whites] food to hire the Abid [slaves].

Makuc Chol Bol, a 17-year-old boy, had just escaped and returned to northern Bahr el-Ghazal when we met him in Tuic County in 1999. He had been in captivity for some four years. He described the incident in which he was abducted:

When the attack came and my whole village ran in disarray, I took to running with my older brother and my uncle. The sounds of gunfire, dogs barking, people shouting and children crying was all just maddening, and no one knew which direction was safe to run towards. The horseback Arab attackers had actually come from the southern end of the village, where they would be least expected to come from. When we ran, some people managed to hide behind the bush or jumped in the river to cross to the other side. Some people were shot dead right then and there. One of the raiders caught me, and with a number of others, we were chained and marched north, through the forest with no water and no food on a three-day journey. As soon as we got into the Arab territory, all the different raiders took any number of abductees they desired and went whichever direction their home village was. I was taken to the town of Meiram and sold to one Yussif Ibrahim, for whom I became a slave for four years. For the first year I wore the same rags I had on when I was taken until they fell apart completely, and that was when Yussif gave me his old gown to tear it apart and pieced it together into a pair of shorts and that was the only piece of cloth I would have for the next several months. I had doubts that I would ever leave that place and to see my family again. While I was there, for nearly a year, I woke up every morning hoping that it would be different day and something or someone would free me from the bondage. I worked so hard everyday hoping that Yussif would either like me for my hard work and treat me like his son, or would let me go. But the harder I worked, the more reliant on me he became and he would treat

of an instrument that would allow the victims and their families to seek justice, and for a declaration that slavery be considered a war crime and a crime against humanity. This is because Sudan's slavery was practiced in the course of a civil war and as a war tactic. These voices were not heeded by the mediators and the warring parties alike partly because negotiated settlements hardly ever end up restoring justice to the victims, as the mediators cannot insist on establishment of such mechanisms lest they risk losing the negotiating momentum. The parties to the conflict were also reluctant to build into the agreement a legal instrument that might be used against them. The result is that Sudan's slaves might not see justice after all. An international criminal court for Sudan was suggested by the European Union and human rights organizations to look into the various violations in Sudan's wars, including slavery, but the proposal was opposed by the United States, and Sudan's military authorities, responsible for some of the gravest violations, will probably go free (see Human Rights Watch 2005).

Bibliography

Collins, Robert (1992), "Nilotic Slavery," in Elizabeth Savage (ed.), *Human Commodity* (London: Frank Cass).

Human Rights Watch (2005), *US Thwarts Justice for Darfur: For Bush Administration, Blocking ICC Trumps Protecting Civilians*. Brussels: Human Rights Watch.

Idris, Amir (2001), *Sudan's Civil War: Slavery, Race and Formational Identities*. Lewiston, NY: Edwin Mellen Press.

Johnson, Douglas (2002), *The Root Causes of Sudan's Civil Wars*. Oxford: James Currey.

Jok, Jok Madut (2001), *War and Slavery in Sudan*. Philadelphia: University of Pennsylvania Press.

Contributors

Kwame Anthony Appiah is Laurance S. Rockefeller University Professor of Philosophy at Princeton University.

Kevin Bales is Professor of Sociology at Roehampton University London and president of Free the Slaves, Washington, DC.

Arnab K. Basu is associate professor of economics and public policy at the College of William and Mary and senior fellow at the Center for Development Research (ZEF), University of Bonn.

Martin Bunzl is professor of philosophy at Rutgers University.

Nancy H. Chau is associate professor of applied economics and management at Cornell University and senior fellow at the Center for Development Research (ZEF), University of Bonn.

Jonathan Conning is associate professor of economics at Hunter College and the Graduate Center of the City University of New York.

Lisa D. Cook is assistant professor of economics at Michigan State University.

Stanley Engerman is John H. Munro Professor of Economics and Professor of History at the University of Rochester.

Jok Madut Jok is associate professor of history at Loyola Marymount University.

Dean S. Karlan is assistant professor of economics at Yale University.

Margaret M. R. Kellow is associate professor of history at University of Western Ontario.

Michael Kevane is associate professor of economics at Santa Clara University.

Alan B. Krueger is Bendheim Professor of Economics and Public Affairs at Princeton University.

E. Ann McDougall is professor of history and classics at University of Alberta.

Howard McGary is professor of philosophy at Rutgers University.

Index

abduction, in Sudan, 149, 152, 153, 154–57, 260, 265. *See also* slavery
abolitionism, 200–211, 213, 217, 227, 254
Adrar region, 166
affection, relations of, 237.
   See also empathy
Africa, 37, 38, 45, 84, 92, 95, 97
African Americans: after emancipation, 88, 89, 90–91; inferior status of, 255; movement north by, 90; payments for freedom by, 200; and redemption, 3; and redemption debate, 201, 202, 204, 205, 206–9; and slavery, 78, 81, 83–84
age, 44, 46, 66, 83
agency, 246, 247
agriculture: in Africa, 92; child labor in, 38, 42, 49, 62, 64, 66, 67, 68, 70; after emancipation, 87, 88, 89, 90, 91; forced labor in, 259; and involuntary contracts, 113; and model of labor and tenancy, 114–22; and output collapse following emancipation, 130; and Russian serfs, 188–89; stigmatization of labor in, 255; in Sudan, 148; in United States, 88, 89. *See also* plantations
akoa/nkoa, 250–51, 252, 253
Akol, Atem Garang, 261–63
akyere, 251–52
Albania, 66
Alexander II, 189–90
Al-Maali, Babikir, 264
Alpers, Edward, 97
altruism, 242, 245
American Anti-Slavery Group (AASG), 144, 145, 146
American Anti-Slavery Society (AASS), 203, 208, 211, 213, 214
American Civil War, 200
American Colonization Society, 201–2
American Revolution, 200, 201, 211
Americas, 86, 88, 91, 94, 97, 103, 113, 119, 122, 181, 195, 249, 250
Amnesty International, 144
Anscombe, Elizabeth, 232
Antigua, 87

Anti-Slavery Society of France, 162, 163
Antony, Yao, 252
Arabs, 147, 149, 151, 160, 256, 260, 265
Argentina, 45
Aristotle, 232, 237, 256
Asante/Ashanti, 101, 249–54
Asia, 37, 38, 45, 95, 97, 130
asset inequality, 128–33, 134
asylum, 43, 61, 73
Atlantic trade, 249, 250
Augustine, W. R., 181
Auld, Hugh, 214, 227, 231
Auld, Thomas, 214, 230
Australia, 45
awowa, 251, 252
Aztecs, 97

Baggara, 34, 147–48, 149, 265
Bahr el-Ghazal, 149, 150, 152, 154, 155, 259
Baier, Annette, 233
Baland, Jean Marie, 110, 135
Bales, Kevin, 15
Banaji, D. R., 96–97
Bangladesh, 45, 66
Barbados, 87
bargaining power: and child labor, 43, 63, 67, 70, 71, 73; and slavery, 24, 215. *See also* labor unions
Barrow, R. H., 96
Basic Human Functional Capabilities, 78
Basu, Arnab K., 39, 42, 61, 64, 70
Basu, Kaushik, 110, 135
Batson, C. Daniel, 239
Bauer, Arnold J., 113
Baum, Gerhardt, 144
Beecher, Henry Ward, 205, 210
Belgium, 39
Belize, 45
Benin, 66
Berkowitz, Leonard, 242
Bhutan, 45, 66
Bibb, Henry, 205
Bîro, Casper, 144
Black Codes, 127–28